SIR GUY BOWED TO ANNETTE

A LITTLE MAID
OF
OLD NEW YORK

BY
ALICE TURNER CURTIS

AUTHOR OF
A LITTLE MAID OF OLD PHILADELPHIA
A LITTLE MAID OF MARYLAND

ILLUSTRATED BY ELIZABETH PILSBRY

APPLEWOOD BOOKS
BEDFORD, MASSACHUSETTS

Paper/S
CuR
1/09

A Little Maid of Old New York was first published by the Penn
Publishing Company in 1921.

ISBN 1-55709-326-1

Thank you for purchasing an Applewood Book.
Applewood reprints America's lively classics—
books from the past that are still of interest to modern readers.
For a free copy of our current catalog, write to:
Applewood Books, Box 365, Bedford, MA 01730.

10 9 8 7 6 5 4 3

Printed and bound in Canada.

Library of Congress Cataloging-in-Publication Data
Curtis, Alice Turner.
   A little maid of old New York / by Alice Turner Curtis, author
of A little maid of old Philadelphia [and] A little maid of
Maryland; illustrated by Elizabeth Pilsbry.
       p.   cm.
   Summary: Ten-year-old Annette finds a way to prove her
loyalty as a good American during the British occupation of
New York City in the Revolutionary War.
   ISBN 1-55709-326-1
   1. New York (N.Y.)—History—Revolution, 1775–1783—
Juvenile fiction.   [1. New York (N.Y.)—History—Revolution,
1775–1783—Fiction.   2. United States—History—Revolution,
1775–1783—Fiction.]
I. Pilsbry, Elizabeth, ill.   II. Title.
PZ7.C941Lmi   1996
[Fic]–dc20   95-49343
                                             CIP
                                             AC

Introduction

THIS story of "A Little Maid of Old New York" tells of the time when British soldiers were in control of that city, and describes the adventures of a loyal little American girl, Annette Vincent, and the Tory girl who was her dearest friend.

The account of Annette's first meeting with Sir Guy Carleton, Washington's entering New York, and the incident connected with the British and American flags should interest deeply the young readers. Girls and boys alike will admire the courage of Annette, and of her sailor cousin John Van Arsdale who raised the American flag on the Battery flagstaff.

Contents

Illustrations

A Little Maid of Old New York

CHAPTER I

A PICNIC PARTY

IT was a pleasant June morning in 1783, and the square brick house, where Annette Vincent lived, on Cherry Street, New York, was flooded with sunshine. The front door was in the centre of the house with two windows on each side; and on the second floor there were five front windows facing the street. There were also five upper windows on the back that overlooked the garden which sloped down to the East River.

It was a fine garden. The path to the river was bordered by thrifty growing box; there were locust trees in blossom; a tall elm, whose branches gave a pleasant shade, stood near the house, and flourishing rose trees, now in full bloom, grew along the wall which separated the garden from that of the neighboring house.

Beside the many flowers and shrubs there was a well-cared-for plot of vegetables, where Mrs. Vincent often worked in the early morning. But Annette was not thinking of the garden on that June morning as she leaned from one of the upper windows and looked anxiously toward the river. She could hear Lottie, her mother's negro maid, singing about her work in the rear of the house. Now and then the rumble of a passing cart on Cherry Street could be heard, and there were calls of birds from the garden. But the sounds were all those of a quiet, peaceful morning, and there was nothing to remind the little American girl that the city of New York had been occupied for nearly seven years by British soldiers whose officers lived in the fine houses on Broadway and Wall Street, while the Bowery, on the outskirts of the city, was occupied by the camps of the British soldiers.

Annette was only ten years old, and she could not remember the days of 1776, before the great fire that destroyed hundreds of buildings, and when General George Washington had been driven from the city by the superior forces of the English under Sir Henry Clinton. But the little girl had often heard those days described by her mother and father. How Sir Henry Clinton had landed his men at Kip's Bay, and, taking the American troops at disadvantage, had put them to rout, pursuing the fugitives over the fields to Murray Hill, and forcing Washington to retreat into New Jersey. But at Yorktown in 1781 the Americans had defeated the English forces under Cornwallis, with the result that the English owned themselves defeated in their struggle to control the United States, and now the loyal Americans of New York believed the time to be near at hand when peace between England and America would be established. Annette was very sure that some day she would see General Washington come riding through the city to Bowling Green and watch the British ships sail from New York harbor with all the English sailors on board.

As she looked eagerly toward the river, watching for the first glimpse of her Cousin John Van Arsdale's sailboat, Annette thought to herself that she wished it might come to pass on this very day. "It would indeed be even better than a picnic at Staten Island to see all those English ships sail away," thought Annette.

Nevertheless the prospect of a sail across the harbor and a picnic dinner with her three best friends, Delia Davidson, Betty Mason, and Katherine Down and Cousin John, was full of delight; and Annette was all ready to run toward the landing at the foot of the garden when she should see the sail of the *Fleetwing*, her cousin's boat, round the point a short distance up the river.

Annette was always very proud indeed when her Cousin John asked her to go with him on one of his frequent excursions about the harbor. John, as Annette often reminded Kathy Down, was a "real sailor," although not yet sixteen years old; he had voyaged to Cuba, beside visiting Jamestown, and other southern ports; and now hoped that the British would soon leave New York and that he might embark on a longer voyage than he had yet undertaken.

John, on his part, was always well pleased with his little cousin's company. She did not jump about in the boat, or meddle with the tiller or the ropes. She was not easily frightened, and obeyed promptly John's careful directions for her safety. To-day was a special occasion; for John had told Annette that she might ask her three girl friends to go with them for a day's picnic to Staten Island. Delia, Betty and Kathy had accepted the invitation with evident enthusiasm, and they were to be at the Battery at an early hour, as that was a more convenient point for them than the landing on Cherry Street.

"There's the boat! There's the *Fleetwing*," Annette exclaimed, as, after a long watchful half hour, she caught her first glimpse of her cousin's boat rounding the point at the foot of the garden; and in an instant the little girl was running down the stairs and through the lower hall to the back porch where her mother sat sewing.

"Here is your cape, dear; and Lottie will carry the basket to the landing," said Mrs. Vincent, smiling at the sight of her little daughter's happy face. "Tell John to take great care of his passengers, and bring you all home in good season."

"Yes, yes, Mother dear. You know Cousin John is never careless. Does not Father say that John could navigate a ship if need were," responded Annette, and the little girl kissed her mother's cheek, and with a smiling "good-bye" ran down the box-bordered path to the river, while Lottie with the well-filled lunch basket followed closely behind her.

They reached the landing some minutes before the *Fleetwing*, and Lottie set the basket down carefully with a warning look toward Annette.

"Yo' sees how keerful I sets this basket down? Wal, den, yo' take keer dat odder folks be keerful wid it," cautioned Lottie. "An' 'sides dat yo' be keerful wid dat clean dress yo's wearin'. Nebber min' if it don' be yo' bes' dress, it be clean," added Lottie solemnly; and Annette promised to be careful, looking down at the pretty blue checked gingham, and thinking to herself that not even Kathy Down, whose father had one of the finest shops on Smith Street (where the wives and daughters of the British officers bought fine lawns and cambrics, silk aprons, and buttons of silver), could have a better-ironed gingham or one made more neatly than this. Annette was always well pleased with the simple dresses her mother made for her. Loyal Americans living in New York in 1783 could not have many fine clothes or luxuries of any kind, and Annette's mother and father had not faltered in their loyalty to America.

Annette's eyes were brown, nearly the same color as a ripe chestnut; and her hair was a shade darker, soft and fine, and hung in smooth curls under her wide hat of coarse white straw which was tied under her chin by a wide blue and white plaided ribbon. She wore white stockings and ankle-tie slippers, and as she stood under the wide spreading oak tree that shaded the landing she made a most pleasant picture.

"Passengers all aboard for Staten Island," John called smilingly, as he skilfully brought the *Fleetwing* beside the landing, and held the boat steady for his cousin to step on board.

"Yo' handle dat basket keerful, Massa John," warned Lottie, as John reached for the square, well-covered basket.

"Of course I will, Lottie," responded John gravely, greatly to the approval of the anxious Lottie, who now turned back to the house sure that her excellent spiced cake would not be broken to bits by careless handling.

"Good and heavy," said John as he set the basket in the tiny cabin.

"There is everything you like best in that basket," declared Annette soberly, as she carefully took the seat John pointed out near the tiller.

"No wonder then that it is heavy," said the boy laughing; "but I'll wager it will be light enough when we come back. A good sail gives a good appetite, and there's a fair breeze this morning. I hope your girl friends will not keep us waiting at the Battery."

"I am sure they will be there before us," Annette replied eagerly. "Kathy Down was at my house yesterday to show me her fine new necklace of coral beads, and she said she would surely be at the Battery in good season."

John was busy with sail and tiller, and made no response to his cousin until the boat had cleared the landing and was headed toward the Battery. Then, as the sail of the *Fleetwing* caught the breeze and the sloop moved swiftly along, he said: "Kathy Down's father is too good a friend of the Tories to suit me, Annette. Why, he says openly that the British officers are his best customers. How happens it that so loyal a girl as you chooses the daughter of such a man for your best friend?" and John looked down at his little cousin as if she were in some way to blame for Mr. Down's opinion of the English officers.

" 'Tis not Kathy's fault that her father is friendly with the British," responded Annette earnestly. "And, Cousin John, how can I help but like her? She is always pleasant, and if you do but look at her she smiles as if she were pleased. Why, my mother says that Kathy has the prettiest manners of any little girl who comes to see me," and Annette looked pleadingly toward her cousin as if hoping he would relent and say that Kathy Down was not to be blamed for the opinions of her father.

But the boy's face did not lose its look of disapproval. He realized, as it was not possible for Annette to do, all the sacrifices and sufferings that had been endured by the loyal Americans of New York during the past seven years while the British officers and their families had taken the best houses in the city for their own use, and passed their time in a round of gayety. It was well known that Daniel Down kept his best goods for their purchase, and received many favors from the officers. He knew that Kathy often played with the English children, and he was sorry that his cousin was so fond of her. But John was too

fair-minded and friendly a lad to cherish any unkindness toward a child, and his face softened as he nodded toward Annette and said: "I must try and be as
well-mannered as Katherine, I suppose, and smile
whenever anyone looks at me."

Annette's face brightened at her cousin's good-
natured response. She was now sure that there would
be no cloud on the pleasure of the day; for, no matter
what might be thought or said of the loyalty of Mr.
Down, Annette was confident that Kathy was her
"best" friend. There was no other girl who could
think of more pleasant games than Kathy, or who
was more ready to help carry out the plans suggested by her companions. So Annette smiled approvingly at her cousin's friendly words, and then looked
eagerly toward Bowling Green and the Battery,
where the English flag floated from the tall flagstaff.

"There they are, John! All three waiting for us. And
I can see baskets. We shall have a feast, for Lottie
said she had packed a fine luncheon."

John's face brightened, for he was boy enough, in
spite of his long voyages, to be well pleased by the
assurance of well-filled picnic baskets, and he waved
his blue cap at the little group on the wharf.

Betty Mason and Delia Davidson were both two
years older than Annette and Kathy. They were tall
girls for their age, and thought themselves nearly
grown up. They each had blue eyes, and their flaxen
hair was neatly braided and nearly hidden from sight

under hats of coarse straw, similar to the one Annette wore. They wore simple dresses of blue cotton, and as they stood side by side they might have been taken for sisters.

Kathy Down was just behind the two older girls, and not until John had politely handed them to their seats in the boat did she step forward. Kathy and Annette were not only the same age but they were nearly the same size and complexion. Kathy's hair was a little darker than Annette's and her eyes were gray instead of brown. When she smiled there were dimples in each cheek; and the little girl's friendly expression and pleasant manners won her the approving regard of the older people as well as of her own playmates.

Unlike the other girls, Kathy did not wear a broad-rimmed hat or a cotton dress. Her dress was of thin blue wool, the skirt made somewhat shorter than was then worn by small girls, and her blouse was made loose and straight like those worn by sailors, with a wide white collar; her cap, too, was shaped like the cap of a sailor, but it was made of scarlet cloth.

Annette looked admiringly at her little friend as she stepped on board, and even John gave an approving look at "the little Tory's" sailor-like costume, thinking it much more suitable for a day's cruise than the ruffled cotton dresses of his other passengers.

But Betty and Delia had already confided to each other that they thought Kathy's dress "queer." They greatly preferred their own flounced gowns and straw hats, and, besides that, the color of Kathy's cap was exactly the color of the coats of the British officers, a color that even the American children had come to consider as a mark of disloyalty to America. So neither Betty nor Delia felt any admiration for Kathy's appearance, but regarded her with unsmiling eyes as she took her seat beside them.

There were a number of English soldiers loitering about the Battery and they looked at the neat sloop and its passengers with good-natured interest. As John made ready to swing his boat out from the wharf one of the soldiers stepped forward and said pleasantly: "Attend to your tiller, young man, and I'll push your boat clear."

John scowled at the man resentfully, and responded sharply: "I need no help."

The smile vanished from the face of the red-coated soldier and he frowned a little threateningly as he said sharply:

"You need a lesson in good manners, young sir; I've a mind to sink your fine boat and shut you up for a while to teach you your place."

The *Fleetwing* was now out of reach, and John laughed scornfully. "Better be getting ready for your voyage to England," he called back, as the mainsail caught the breeze and sent the boat skimming over the water, leaving a sparkling ripple in her wake.

But the little girls were frightened by the soldier's words, and Annette looked at her cousin anxiously, wishing that John had not shown so plainly his dislike toward the redcoat.

"Could he—could he sink the boat and shut you up, John?" she questioned fearfully.

John nodded carelessly, as if being shut up by an English soldier was a very small matter.

"Oh, very likely. New York is a Tory city, in spite of our army having beaten them at Bunker Hill and Yorktown. But it will not be long before the British will be driven out," he declared, "and I'd like to be the one to pull down their old flag when they do go," he added sharply, turning a revengeful glance back to the tall flagpole on the Battery where the English flag floated in the summer breeze. But John had not the faintest idea that, before six months should pass, he would perform that very service while General Washington looked on.

"I do not believe the English soldier would really—" began Katherine, but John looked at her with such disapproval that the little girl did not venture to continue her excuses for America's enemy, and she turned toward Betty and Delia only to find that they, too, were regarding her in surprise.

Katherine began to wish that she had not accepted Annette's invitation. She wondered why her companions were so silent and unfriendly, and had

Annette not, at that very moment, exclaimed ardently: "Oh, Kathy, you always wear the prettiest things. I wish I had a dress and cap exactly like yours," Kathy would have felt herself quite deserted. But she was ready to smile happily at her little friend, and was about to explain that her mother had made both dress and cap, when Delia said:

"Kathy's cap is the same color as the coats of the British officers. 'Tis not a color I like to see or wear," and Delia looked toward John as if expecting a word of approval for her loyal sentiment.

But John had not heard the remark. He was busy shaping the boat's course, and at that moment he called out:

"Look out for your heads," and as Kathy and Annette leaned over for the boom to swing to leeward Annette whispered: "Kathy, I have something lovely to tell you just as soon as I can without the others hearing." So Katherine was quite her smiling self again, and explained to Delia that her mother had intended making her a cap of blue cloth, but had not enough material.

John was singing softly to himself:

> *"The wind sets fair,*
> *The vessel's stout and tall,*
> *Bright Castabella.*
> *A sailor free from care*
> *Am I, when the wind sets fair,*
> *Bright Castabella,"*

as he guided his boat down the harbor, past the British ships that lay at anchor awaiting the commands of Sir Guy Carleton, who had already promised Governor Clinton that the British soldiers should leave New York as soon as possible.

Beyond the ships the girls could see the pleasant wooded shores of Staten Island, and John headed the *Fleetwing* toward the eastern end of the island, where there was no settlement near the shore, and where he felt sure no one would disturb them.

The place John had selected for a landing was a ledge of rocks that ran out into the deep water. Here the sloop could float easily and would not ground, and the girls could walk from the ledge to the shore without wetting their shoes.

Delia and Betty stepped very carefully as they made their way over the ledge. But Kathy clasped Annette's arm. "I am going to take off my shoes and stockings and leave them in the boat, then I can run about as I please," she said.

"I will too," responded Annette eagerly, with an admiring look at Kathy's smiling face, and the two little girls put their shoes and stockings and also their hats in the tiny cabin.

Delia and Betty looked at the younger girls in surprise as Annette and Kathy ran lightly over the warm brown ledges to the grassy slope where John had carried the baskets. Delia would have been glad to follow their example, but Betty's look was disapproving. Betty felt that she was too nearly a young lady to run about barefooted.

The little point toward the eastern end of the island was the very place for a day's picnic. There was a smooth, grass-grown slope, well shaded by a large beech-tree. Behind this was thick undergrowth and tall trees. Beyond the ledge where they had landed stretched a smooth beach, and Katherine promptly suggested to Annette that they should go wading.

"The water is sure to be warm, and then you can tell me what you did not want the others to hear," she said, as the two little girls stood together a short distance from the others.

"That will be splendid," Annette responded quickly. "Betty Mason has begun to knit already, and she and Delia will never miss us. John is spreading a strip of sail-cloth over that old log for them to sit on, and if he wants us, all he has to do is call and we will be sure to hear him."

"Yes, indeed," smiled Kathy, and hand in hand the two little girls ran over the smooth, sun-warmed ledges to the sandy beach.

As they reached the water's edge Annette said: "Now I will tell you, Katherine, and I do hope you will think it as splendid as I do."

CHAPTER II

THERE was no house to be seen from the little point where the *Fleetwing* had landed its passengers. But there were many flourishing farms and settlements on Staten Island, and it had been a place of great importance to both the English and American armies.

"It's not far from here that Lord William Howe landed his thirty thousand troops in August, 1776," said John soberly, as he turned to look out across the harbor where the English men-of-war and other ships of the enemy floated at anchor.

"And those very soldiers landed at Kip's Bay and drove the American army from New York," said Betty gravely, looking up from the stocking of white cotton that she was knitting. "Mother remembers all about it," she continued. "She says that there were swarms of British troops everywhere."

"Of course she remembers it; I remember it myself, and I always shall," responded John. "Why, 'tis but seven years ago. And 'twill not be as many months longer now before we'll see these British ships, with all their redcoats on board, sail out of New York harbor forever, and Washington in New York to stay."

23

"Then my father will come home, for he is with General Washington," said Betty happily. "But are you very sure, John, that the English will soon leave New York?" she added, a little doubtful that such good news could be true.

John nodded confidently. "They can't stay much longer," he declared. "Why, 'tis nearly two years since the Americans drove Cornwallis from Yorktown, and everyone said that ended the war and made America a free nation. But these English stay on here until the United States and England can agree on a Treaty of Peace."

Delia and Betty exchanged a puzzled look. Neither of the girls quite understood what John meant by the word "treaty," but both were sure it had something to do with the return of General Washington to New York, and therefore it must be an excellent word. Neither of them wished to ask John to explain it, so Delia said: "Yes indeed," as if agreeing with what John had said, and Betty began counting stitches with great diligence.

" 'Tis too early for lunch," said John, a little regretfully, with a glance at the well-filled baskets. " 'Tis not much after ten. I will sail along shore for an hour and maybe catch a cod or two. You girls will not be afraid to be left alone?"

"No, indeed," Betty and Delia answered promptly. "Annette and Kathy are running about on the beach within call, and will soon return, and we will begin to spread the luncheon when we see the *Fleetwing* headed for shore," continued Betty.

"I'll not be away more than an hour or two," said John, "unless one of these British ships captures the *Fleetwing*," he added laughingly, and turned back toward his boat, well pleased at the prospect of a further cruise along the winding shore.

Betty and Delia watched John as he ran swiftly over the ledges, and in a few moments they saw the *Fleetwing* move slowly out into the channel; then Betty returned to her knitting. But Delia drew a long breath of satisfaction.

"Goody! Goody! Goody!" she exclaimed, jumping about, to Betty's evident amazement. "I hope he will stay away for hours, don't you, Betty?"

"What for?" exclaimed Betty. "I am sure John is a kind and pleasant boy, and 'tis not polite or seemly to wish him away when we would not be here at all save for his kindness," and Betty looked disapprovingly at her friend.

"Oh! Of course, Betty, I do not mean any harm of John; only I feared he might think I was too nearly grown up to take off my shoes and stockings and play with Kathy and Annette as I mean to," and Delia began untying her shoes as she spoke.

"Well, Delia, it does seem like a little girl to wish to do so foolish a thing," Betty replied disapprovingly. "I am very sure I would not think of it even."

"You are only twelve anyway, Betsy Mason," Delia

reminded her, "and I am sure there is no harm in taking off one's hat and shoes and stockings on so warm a day. Oh! Betty, come on. You will have years and years to be grown up," and Delia looked pleadingly at Betty's sober face.

For a moment Betty made no reply. She was just "setting the heel" of the stocking, and was carefully counting stitches. Delia was in no mood to wait patiently, and as she untied the broad hat ribbons she exclaimed:

"Well, sit there and knit then, if that is your idea of a picnic. I am going to find Annette and Kathy and have a good time. I'm not in such a hurry to be an old woman as you are, Betty Mason," and with a scornful look at her companion, Delia started off toward the shore.

The grass was not as soft as Delia had expected, and after a few steps she began to go more cautiously. But once on the smooth ledge she quickened her pace. She could see Annette and Kathy wading in the quiet waters of the cove and was eager to join them.

Annette had told Kathy the pleasant news that she had not wished the other girls to hear, and Kathy was as well pleased as Annette had hoped. Annette's news was an invitation for Katherine to accompany her on a visit to her Grandmother Vincent, who lived in Greenwich Village.

"My grandmother told me to ask any little girl I pleased for company," Annette had explained eagerly, "and I would rather have you than anyone, Kathy.

She wishes us to come next Saturday and stay a week, and my father will drive us there and come after us."

"I am sure my mother will be well pleased that I have so kind an invitation," said Katherine, smiling so radiantly that Annette thought, as she so often did, that there was no other girl in all New York as lovely or as friendly as Kathy Down. Before either of the little girls could say another word a loud call made them turn quickly, to see Delia running along the beach toward them.

"Isn't it fun to wade!" she called eagerly, splashing along at the edge of the shore. "Betty wouldn't come. She'd rather make-believe she is grown up," Delia added, as she came up beside the younger girls. "I wish we all had on old dresses, then we could splash about all we liked," she said regretfully, holding up well-starched skirts with both hands. "John has gone off shore fishing," she added.

"And our shoes and stockings and hats are in the *Fleetwing's* cabin," exclaimed Katherine.

"That's no matter," Annette hastened to assure her friend. "We will not want to put them on until we start for home."

"Isn't there some game we can play?" questioned Delia. "I think it would be fun to play 'Indians.' We could capture Betty and make her think we really were Indians."

"How could we do that? We haven't any blankets or feathers, or anything to hide our dresses," responded

Kathy, laughing at the idea that Betty could be so easily deceived as to take them for Indians.

"Come up the beach a little way and I will tell you just how," Delia replied soberly, leading the way to dry land, closely followed by Annette and Kathy, who looked at their companion wonderingly.

"I can tell you just how we could dress up so that no one would ever know us," said Delia. "We could fasten leaves and brakes all over our dresses, and make head-dresses of leaves to cover our heads, and I'm sure we can stain our hands and faces with bits of chestnut bark."

As Delia described her plan her face grew eager, and Annette and Kathy both began to think it would be great fun to dress up in leaves and play "Indian," but they were still doubtful about capturing Betty.

"What would we do with her?" asked Annette.

"Oh, just lead her into the woods and leave her. Then she would call and we would pull off our disguise and run to rescue her, and Betty would tell us that Indians had bound her and taken her to the woods. Afterwards we would tell her all about it. It would be a great joke on Betty," and Delia smiled at the thought of her friend's surprise.

"You see," she continued, "we won't let Betty really see us. We can creep up behind that log and blindfold her—"

"What with?" interrupted Annette. "If we use any of our things Betty will know who it is right away."

"WE CAN CREEP ALONG AT THE EDGE OF THE WOODS"

Delia shook her head. "Oh, no, she will be too surprised. I can twist my sash about her head so quickly that she won't have a glimpse of it, and you and Kathy can tie her hands together with your handkerchiefs. We won't speak, we will just lead her off in silence. Come on, let's begin to get leaves," and Delia ran to the sloping bank and began to break off small branches of oak.

Annette and Kathy followed her, and in a short time the three girls were busy fastening garlands of leaves together with small twigs. It was an easy matter to make head-dresses of leaves and of the tall green brakes that grew in such quantities a short distance from the shore; but they found it a more difficult matter to cover their skirts with leaves held together by twigs, and finally decided that small branches of maple and birch leaves tied about their waists, with others held about their shoulders by twisted grass, would disguise them sufficiently, as Delia assured the younger girls that Betty would not see them at all.

"We must hurry and capture her before the *Fleetwing* gets back," said Delia. "We can creep along at the edge of the woods. We may have to say, 'Fear not,' way down in our throats, so Betty will not be too frightened."

"Betty is never frightened," Annette declared. "I heard her say that she would not be afraid of the whole British army."

"Well, of course she wouldn't. The whole British army would not hurt one little girl," Kathy responded quickly, "but being captured by Indians is different. We must not let Betty be *really* frightened," and Kathy looked at Delia a little doubtfully.

But the older girl cheerfully agreed with both Annette and Kathy. "Of course Betty won't be really frightened, and it is a good chance to find out if she is truly as brave as she pretends," she said quickly, as she looked at her companions to make sure that their costumes of leaves and brakes was a sufficient disguise.

"Now we will creep along at the edge of the woods and come up behind the log as softly as possible." she continued. "I will have my sash all ready, and I will bind it over her face and at the same time you girls must tie her hands."

"Yes! Yes!" agreed Annette and Kathy.

"Then we will lead her into the woods a little way and leave her, and hide and see what she will do," continued Delia.

"But if she is really frightened we must let her know quickly that it is only a game," said Annette, and Delia promptly consented; but the older girl thought to herself that both Annette and Kathy were rather silly to insist that Betty should not be seriously frightened. Delia considered that in playing "Indians" half the fun was that the captured should believe themselves in danger.

"Come on," said Delia in a husky whisper, "and if you hurt your feet on the stubbly grass, don't call out," and with cautious steps she led the way back to the little clearing. But not by the way of the smooth ledges where Betty might see their approach. Delia crept along close to the thickly growing bushes near the shore, and Annette and Kathy followed closely behind her.

The three girls endeavored to walk as much like Indians as possible. Every few steps Delia would stop and look cautiously around as if they might be discovered by unseen enemies. Then she would nod to her followers and move on.

The log where Betty had seated herself was screened by a growth of laurel bushes, and it was behind these that the "Indians" stopped for a moment's rest.

"Now creep silently," whispered Delia, "and follow me," and she stepped out close to the log where she had left Betty so short a time ago.

Delia stopped suddenly and looked about as if she feared she had come to the wrong place, and Annette and Kathy also stared about with wondering eyes.

For Betty was not to he seen. There was the log covered with the strip of sail-cloth, and there lay Betty's hat and the stocking on which she had been knitting, but Betty and the lunch-baskets had vanished.

CHAPTER III

FOR a moment the girls looked at each other in amazement, then Delia whispered:

"Sshh—don't speak out loud. Betty is close by."

"But where?" responded Annette.

"Wait a minute; she is surely not far away, said Delia, confidently, and the three little girls again crouched silently behind the log where Betty's hat and work rested. Now and then one of them would cautiously raise her head and peer anxiously about, but there was no sign of Betty, and they were all becoming a little tired of so discouraging a game when a loud shout made them all spring up suddenly to find John standing in the middle of the clearing looking about as if he could not understand what had happened to his companions.

"Oh, here you are!" he declared with evident relief. "But you look like small trees walking," he added, smiling at the girls' head-dresses of nodding brakes and the leafy branches that hid their dresses.

"Where is my luncheon?" he continued, looking about as if expecting to see it spread out on the grassy slope.

33

"Oh! The baskets are gone too!" exclaimed Annette in surprise, as she looked in vain for the well-filled luncheon baskets.

"Gone too?" questioned John, and then quickly realized that Betty was missing. Before he could ask a question Annette began to tell him of the game they had planned, and of their discovery that Betty had disappeared.

John's face was very grave when the little girl had finished her story.

"I see! And while you girls were making ready to take Betty prisoner for a game she really was captured by Indians. They may have been lurking near when we landed, and noticed the luncheon baskets, and seeing Betty alone they thought it too good a chance to miss," said John, adding: "It's my fault. I ought to have stayed on shore."

"It's *my* fault!" declared Delia, evidently ready to cry. "I ought to have stayed with Betty."

But John shook his head. "Then there would be two girls missing instead of one," he said. "But we must do our best to find Betty. Perhaps they have not taken her very far. Probably the baskets of food is what they wanted, and they may have left Betty near here. They would not want to be bothered with a small girl."

For a moment the little group looked at each other with anxious eyes. They forgot everything except the possibility that Betty might have been taken by some wandering band of Indians, many of whom still lurked about the islands and unsettled country near New York, often ready to commit mischief, and they were feared by the settlers in lonely places.

Although John endeavored not to let the little girls know how seriously he was alarmed by Betty's disappearance, Annette was quick to see that her cousin was worried and anxious.

"What can we do to find Betty?" she asked.

For a moment John made no answer. He realized that he was responsible for the safety of Annette, Delia and Kathy, as well as for Betty's return, but he had learned the importance of deciding promptly, and it did not take him long to make a plan.

"First of all I must take you girls on board the *Fleetwing*," he said, moving toward the ledge. "If I leave you here the Indians may return, and you cannot travel through these woods."

Delia had begun pulling on her stockings, and she picked up her own hat and Betty's, as well as Betty's knitting, before following the others toward the boat.

"Can't we help at all, John?" Annette pleaded, as John pushed the sloop out from shore. But John was busy with rope and tiller and made no answer. He was thinking of old stories of the Weckquaeskeeck Indians who had taken white children into captivity. Some way he must rescue Betty from such a fate.

His plan was to anchor the *Fleetwing* at some distance from shore, then paddle back in the small rowboat and endeavor to find trace of the missing girl.

As he anchored the sloop, John told the girls what he meant to do.

"You will be safe here, and can watch the shore. If you see any signs of Indians, or if Betty should come to the shore, you will see her, and in either case, if it be Betty or Indians, you must all call my name as loudly as you can. I will do my best to find Betty, and I may have to get some of the settlers to help me."

The three girls listened with grave faces, and as John pushed off from the sloop in the small boat they promised to follow his directions and to call if either Betty or Indians should appear on the shore.

They watched him land and draw the skiff up under the thickly growing trees near the shore where it could not easily be seen, and then John vanished from sight.

"I ought to have stayed with Betty," said Delia, in so doleful a voice that Kathy quickly slipped her arm about the elder girl and said:

"But, Delia, perhaps if you had not come to the beach the Indians would have captured all of us."

"I don't believe it was Indians," declared Annette. "I believe it was British soldiers."

The other two girls looked at their friend in amazement, and Kathy said quickly:

"Then Betty is safe! If the British soldiers carried her away with the baskets they are sure to have done it for a joke, and will bring her back," and Kathy smiled as if quite sure Delia and Annette must agree with her that it was not at all dangerous to be carried off by the soldiers of King George.

But her smile quickly faded when Delia drew away and exclaimed: "Well, Katherine Down! I suppose you think it's all right to steal our luncheon and frighten poor Betty, so long as your friends the British soldiers are the ones to blame," and Kathy found that even the faithful Annette was looking at her with disapproving eyes. But before either of the little girls could speak they heard the splash of oars and a loud call, and turned to see a long boat manned by red-coated soldiers drawing up beside the *Fleetwing*. It had evidently come around the point and the girls had been watching the shore so intently that they had not noticed it.

For a moment the girls gazed at the young man who had leaped lightly from the boat into the *Fleetwing*, as if they were too frightened to speak, but as he turned and lifted Betty on board they all called out joyfully: "Oh, Betty! Betty! Betty!" and for the moment forgetting the hated soldiers, smiled happily at their friend.

Betty began talking before they could ask her a question. "I got lost," she declared. "After you started off, Delia, I thought I would just walk into the woods a little way, and I kept walking, and first thing I knew I came to another shore! And these kind men were fishing quite near, and when they saw me they came and got me, and I told them about the ledge and the cove and the smooth grassy place, and they were just bringing me back when I saw you were all on the *Fleetwing*. Where's John?" And Betty, a little breathless, but smiling happily, looked about for some sign of the *Fleetwing*'s captain.

At Betty's question the other girls recalled John's command to call him at the moment Betty should appear, and instantly Annette, Delia and Kathy called: "John! John! John!" greatly to the amusement of the red-coated soldier who had lifted Betty on board the *Fleetwing*.

There were two other men in the rowboat, who laughed heartily as the girls' voices rang out across the quiet cove and then were echoed in fainter notes—"John! John! John!" until it seemed as if a dozen voices were calling.

"Come on, Peter," called one of the oarsmen, "we must get back to our fishing."

"I don't like leaving these children alone," said Peter, but his companions urged him impatiently, and just as John appeared on the ledge Peter stepped into the boat.

"Thank you very much for bringing me to the *Fleetwing*," said Betty, looking up at the friendly young soldier.

"You are quite welcome," he responded smilingly, "but in future don't leave your friends when you are on a strange island."

"Oh, they left me," Betty explained eagerly.

"We are all much obliged to you, Mr. Peter," Annette added, remembering that it was her party, and therefore her duty to thank Betty's rescuers, even if they were English soldiers, "and to your friends," she added, looking at the two red-coated men who held their oars ready to start.

The men nodded in friendly fashion, and one of them said: "You are a very polite little lady; perhaps your father is an Englishman?"

"Oh, no indeed, he is a loyal American," Annette answered quickly.

"Come on, Peter, before you are captured by the enemy," said the man, still smiling, and the young soldier jumped lightly into the boat, and the men dipped their oars, and called back a good-bye to the little group on board the *Fleetwing* as their skiff moved swiftly across the quiet water toward the point.

John had come racing back to the shore at the sound of the girls' voices just in time to see the boat with three red-coated soldiers on board moving away from his sloop. In a moment he had pulled his skiff from its hiding-place and was rowing toward the *Fleetwing*. John did not stop to think that these English soldiers might decide to take him a prisoner, or that he could do little to prevent their taking possession of his boat if they decided to; he thought only of the four small girls for whose safety he was responsible, and was ready to face any number of red-coats in their behalf; nevertheless he was glad to see their boat headed toward the point.

As John drew near the sloop Annette called out: "Betty is safe. She got lost and the soldiers found her and brought her back," and Betty added:

"They were just as kind as if they had been American soldiers."

John made no response to this. He was thankful indeed to have Betty safe on board the *Fleetwing*.

"Where are the lunch-baskets?" Betty asked a moment later, looking about as if expecting to see them.

"They are lost!" declared Delia. "Someone must have taken them, Betty, after you went away, for we could not see them."

"Of course you couldn't. I set them behind the laurel bushes," responded Betty.

"I'll fetch them on board," said John, "and we will eat our luncheon here. It is well past noon now."

The little girls looked at one another with sober faces, and John was quick to see that they were disappointed, and added: "Perhaps it will be more fun to go on shore after all," and began to pull up the anchor.

The girls' faces brightened instantly. "Yes indeed. It wouldn't seem like a real picnic to eat luncheon on the boat," said Annette.

John hoisted the sail and turned the *Fleetwing*'s prow toward the ledge.

Betty was the first to land, and she ran swiftly along the ledge to the clearing and was bringing the baskets from their hiding-place when the other girls joined her.

It was now well on in the afternoon, and they were all hungry. As they sat about the big log and ate the excellent food John gravely reminded them that they all ought to be grateful indeed that no wandering band of Indians had found Betty and carried her away.

"And that the soldiers found me," said Betty, adding soberly: "I do not see why they are not just like Americans."

"I will be well pleased when there's not a red-coat to be seen within a day's sail of New York," said John, "and we must be starting for home. The wind is offshore now, and 'twill take longer to get back than it did to come."

The little girls took their places in the boat, talking eagerly of all that had happened since they first landed on the ledge. Delia felt that Betty was the heroine of the day; to be lost and rescued by British soldiers seemed a great adventure. Annette and Kathy, seated near the tiny cabin, whispered together of the good time they were sure to have when they visited Madame Vincent at Greenwich Village, while John whistled softly to himself as he watched the English warships lying at anchor, and hoped that very soon he might see them all sail out New York harbor never to return.

"I'm sure we will always remember our picnic at Staten Island," said Delia, as the *Fleetwing* approached the Battery landing.

"Thank you for our lovely sail," said Kathy, as John helped her from the boat. But Betty quite forgot to thank the young sailor; she had started off toward home eager to tell her mother of the great adventure.

"I guess Betty has forgotten all about being grown up," said Delia, as she thanked Annette and John for the day's excursion and followed her friends toward home.

The long June day was nearly over as John sailed the *Fleetwing* along the shore toward the landing at the foot of the Vincent garden. The land breeze brought the fragrance of many flowering shrubs and plants from the pleasant gardens that bordered the harbor's edge, and Annette, watching the glow of the setting sun reflected in the waters of the bay, was sure there was no lovelier place in all the world than her own home.

Mrs. Vincent was at the landing and Annette called out gaily: "Oh, Mother, dear, we have had adventures by sea and land."

John laughed at his little cousin's words, and explained briefly to his aunt just what had happened.

"Make your boat fast and come in to supper with us, John," said Mrs. Vincent, and the boy smilingly complied.

As they walked through the garden Annette told of dressing up in leaves and ferns, and of their plan to capture Betty. "And Kathy has promised to go to Grandma's with me," she added, as they reached the house.

CHAPTER IV

At Annette's words: "Kathy has promised to go to Grandma's with me," John's smile vanished and he looked quickly toward his aunt, wondering if Mrs. Vincent would approve of Annette's invitation to "the little Tory," as he called Kathy in his thoughts. But Mrs. Vincent made no response, and very soon they were all seated about the table in the dining-room, where Annette's father was waiting for them.

As Mr. Vincent listened to Annette's story of the day's adventures his face grew serious.

"Staten Island is not the safest place for loyal Americans just now," he said, "and I should not have been surprised if some of those British soldiers had taken your sloop, John, and left you to get home as best you could. The British have controlled that island since 1776."

"And the Indians, the Delawares and Aquehongas, still lurk about the island," added Mrs. Vincent.

"I chose a safe place," responded John. "The British do not dare trouble Americans much now. They know they are beaten. I heard this very morning that American prisoners are being set free from the

44

Provost Building and from the prison ships in the harbor. I'm not afraid of the British," John concluded.

Mr. Vincent smiled at his nephew's words, and turned toward Annette. "Who is to go with you to Grandma Vincent's on Saturday, Annette?" he questioned.

"Kathy Down, Father. I like Kathy the best of all the girls, and I am sure Grandma will think her a pleasant child," Annette answered.

"It may be that Mrs. Down will not think best for Katherine to go to Greenwich Village," said Mrs. Vincent.

"Oh, Mother!" Annette's voice sounded as if she was ready to cry at even the suggestion of such a thing. But nothing more was said of the visit, and after supper John bade them good-night and returned to his boat to sail up the East River to his own home while the Vincents sat for a while on their front porch to enjoy the cool of the evening and to exchange friendly greetings with their neighbors, as was the pleasant custom of the neighborhood.

"I have been thinking, Annette, that on July Fourth you could ask all your little friends to a garden party," said Mrs. Vincent, as the clock struck nine, and Annette, quite ready for sleep after her long day in the open air, started for bed.

"Oh, Mother, that will be splendid," declared the little girl, "and that will be the very week after we get home from Greenwich Village."

"July Fourth is the day we must remember, even with the British still in New York," said Mr. Vincent, following Annette up the broad staircase, "for it was the date of America's formal Declaration of Independence in 1776."

"Yes, Mother. And what will we do that day?" responded Annette.

"Why, we must plan some entertainment," said Mrs. Vincent. "When you go to Greenwich Village you can ask Grandma Vincent to suggest something that we can do to amuse your little friends."

"Yes, yes, I will. Grandma can always think of lovely games," declared Annette, and long after Mrs. Vincent had said good-night the little girl's thoughts lingered about the good times ahead: the visit to her grandmother, and a garden party to follow. It was no wonder that Annette believed herself a very fortunate girl and quite forgot the possibility that Kathy Down's mother might not give permission for her little daughter to go to Greenwich Village for a visit to Madame Vincent.

It was two days later when Lottie handed a note to Annette, saying: "Dat wuthless nigger ob Massa Down's jes' fetched dis, an' he say 'tis for Miss Annette."

At that time negroes were held as slaves in New York City, and there was an open market where they were bought and sold. It was not until 1827 that slavery in New York ended.

"Oh, it's from Kathy, to say that she will go with me on Saturday morning," Annette exclaimed, as she took the square folded note. But after she had broken the seal and read a few lines her smile disappeared, for Kathy had written to say that her mother would not permit her to accept Annette's invitation.

"I am so sorry, dear Annette," wrote Kathy, "that I cannot go with you on Saturday, but I thank you very much for asking me. I want to see you very much for I have a great secret to tell you. I hope I can see you before you go to Greenwich Village."

"Oh, dear! What will I do? Kathy cannot go with me to Grandma's," said Annette, as she finished reading her letter and turned toward her mother, who was busy with her sewing.

"And I do believe you are glad, Mother" the little girl added. "You look as if you were glad that Kathy cannot go, and I have heard you say that she is a pleasant and well-mannered child."

Mrs. Vincent lay down her work and put her arm about Annette. "So she is, dear; but if Kathy cannot go you can surely ask Delia or Betty."

"No! If Kathy cannot go I will go alone," declared the little girl. "I know why you do not want Kathy to go, and why Cousin John does not like her. 'Tis because her father is friendly with the British. 'Tis not fair, Mother," and Annette's cheeks flushed at the thought that her little friend was not fairly treated. Without giving her mother time to reply Annette ran from the sitting-room into the garden, still holding Kathy's letter in her hand.

She went toward the river to her favorite seat under the big oak tree near the landing, and sitting down on the broad wooden bench that Mr. Vincent had built there, she again opened and read Kathy's letter.

"I do wish I knew what Kathy's great secret is," she thought, "and if I go to Grandma's on Saturday I must see Kathy to-day or to-morrow." Annette's face grew serious at this, for she was almost sure that her mother would not give her permission to go to Mr. Down's fine house on Nassau Street, where two English officers lodged.

"I'll go now," she suddenly decided, and ran back toward the house. Mrs. Vincent had stepped to the kitchen to assist Lottie in some household task, so that Annette reached her own room, put on her pretty hat of white straw and reached the street without being seen. She hurried along, turning into St. George's Square, and crossing Queen Street turned westward to Wall Street, which was then the fashionable promenade of the city. But it was too early in the day to meet any of the fine ladies on their way to Smith Street, where Merchant Down and other shopkeepers displayed camblets, moreens, lute-strings, silks and India muslins, and Annette reached Nassau Street without meeting anyone whom she knew.

The Down house was shaded by two large elm trees, and the front door was reached by a long flight of wooden steps. Annette had been so eager to see Kathy and to endeavor to persuade Mrs. Down to give permission for her little daughter to make the visit to Greenwich Village that she had run nearly all the way from Cherry Street, and she was now warm and tired and stood for a moment at the foot of the steps to rest. As she waited there the big front door swung open and Annette looked up to see Kathy looking down at her.

"I saw you from my chamber window, Annette, and I ran down to open the door for you," said Kathy, smiling down at her little visitor.

"Oh, Kathy," panted Annette, still a little out of breath, "I ran nearly all the way."

Kathy was down the steps in a moment, and putting her arm about Annette, said: "I'll help you up the steps. But why did you run? It is too warm to hurry. I hope you have no ill news?"

Annette did not reply until they had entered the big cool sitting-room and were seated near an open window. Then she said:

"Kathy, I couldn't wait, hardly, to get here. What is the secret? And why will your mother not permit you to go with me to Greenwich Village? Oh, Kathy! We would have such a good time at Grandma Vincent's, and 'twill all be spoiled if you do not go. I mean to ask your mother to say that you may. Do you not think that she will change her mind, Kathy?" and Annette looked pleadingly at her little friend.

Kathy shook her head soberly. "No, Annette. For she bade me not to speak of it again. And Mother is not at home this morning. She has gone for the day to Bloomingdale Village. Can you not spend the day with me, Annette?" she asked eagerly.

But Annette was sure that she could not. Suddenly the little girl realized that, in creeping out of her home without asking her mother's permission to visit Kathy, she had done what her Cousin John would call "a sneaky trick," and her face flushed uncomfortably.

"Oh, Kathy, I must go straight home," she declared, jumping up from the comfortable chair near the window.

"But you have just come. You have not heard my secret. Besides, Phyllis is making a cool drink for us flavored with crushed strawberries, and here she is now," said Kathy, as a smiling negro girl appeared in the open doorway carrying a silver tray holding two tall glasses filled with the cool drink flavored with strawberries, and a plate of small frosted cakes.

A little smile crept over Annette's face as Kathy handed her one of the tall glasses, and she drank thirstily; then, nibbling one of the frosted cakes, she sank back in the chair, quite forgetting for the moment her resolve to hasten home and tell her mother of her visit to Kathy.

Kathy sat down beside her little visitor, well pleased at Annette's decision to remain, and as Phyllis left the room, Kathy said: "My secret is a truly serious secret, Annette," and her face grew sober as she looked at her friend. "And perhaps I ought not even to tell you."

Annette set down the tall shining glass on a little table near by before she spoke, then she said slowly: "We promised to tell each other all our secrets."

"Yes," agreed Kathy, "but you see, this is Father's and Mother's secret too."

"I won't tell. Wild horses couldn't make me," Annette promised.

Kathy leaned toward her friend, and after a sharp look toward the door to make sure that no one was near, she whispered: "We are all going away from New York."

"Oh, Kathy!" exclaimed Annette, thinking that this was the worst news possible.

"Yes," continued Kathy, still whispering, "Father says that very soon the British army will go, and then New York will not be safe. Why, Annette, already he has packed up a good part of his fine things in the shop. And Mother has packed many things in the house."

"But where are you going?" Annette asked, nearly ready to cry at the thought of losing Kathy.

"We are going to a far-off island called Bermuda, as soon as Father can find a small sailing vessel and a crew of trusty men to take us. And that is why I cannot go with you to Greenwich Village on Saturday. Mother did not tell me until yesterday," said Kathy.

"But why is it a secret?" questioned Annette.

Kathy shook her head. "I am not sure, but I think Father is afraid he might not be allowed to go if his plan was known," she replied. "And so, Annette, you must not hurry home, for it may be the last day you can visit me. I may be far away from New York when you return from your visit to Greenwich Village."

For a moment the two little friends looked at each other in silence, then Annette said: "Yes, Kathy, of course I will stay. I will stay all day if you want me to."

"Splendid! Splendid!" exclaimed Kathy, jumping up and smiling with delight. "Mother will not be home until evening, or Father either, and there is no one in the house but Phyllis. We will have a lovely time."

But Annette looked at Kathy with serious eyes. "Oh, Kathy, what will I do when you go to Bermuda?" she said soberly.

But Kathy was too happy at the thought of having Annette as her guest for all the long June day to be troubled by what the future might bring.

"We will not think about that," said Katherine, "for it will be hours and hours before you need start for home, Annette, and we will enjoy every hour. First of all, come up-stairs and see my fine new doll that Sir Guy Carleton gave me only yesterday," and taking Annette by the hand, Kathy started toward the stairway.

CHAPTER V

AN UNEXPECTED VISITOR

"I NAMED the doll the very minute Sir Guy gave it to me," Kathy said eagerly, as the two little friends ran up the broad stairway to Kathy's chamber. "I named her 'Annette Carleton,'" and Kathy looked at her little visitor as if perfectly sure of her delighted approval.

"Oh, Kathy!" responded Annette, smiling happily; for it seemed a very wonderful thing to have a doll named for her. Like many other little girls Annette always selected the finest names she could possibly think of for her dolls. But she wished that her namesake might not have "Carleton" for her other name. Sir Guy Carleton might be a very fine British officer, and Annette knew that he was in command of all the English troops in New York, but to the little American girl this was reason enough for not liking his name. For a moment she was tempted to say that Kathy must choose between changing the doll's last name, or not call it "Annette." But suddenly she remembered what Kathy had told her: that she was going to a far-off island, that this might be their last

day together, and Annette quickly resolved that she
would not do or say an unkind or unfriendly word for
the entire day. So she smiled back at Kathy as her
friend led the way to the broad window-seat where,
in a small armchair covered with crimson silk, "Miss
Annette Carleton" sat in state.

It was the most wonderful doll that Annette had
ever seen. It was much larger than the average doll;
and Kathy explained that Sir Guy had sent to Paris
for it.

"Look," said Kathy proudly, "her arms have joints,
just as ours have," and she moved the doll's arms and
hands that Annette might see this marvel; and then
showed Annette the doll's fine wardrobe that was
neatly packed in a small wooden trunk. There was a
dress of pale yellow silk, with a tiny parasol to
match, and little yellow silk slippers; there was a coat
of white velvet embroidered with gold thread, and a
white bonnet with a tiny wreath of pale blue flowers.
Then there were little lace-bordered handkerchiefs
and underwear. But, most wonderful of all, there
were necklaces of beads for this favored doll to
choose from. Pale amber beads, pearl beads, and
shining blue beads.

As Annette looked at all these treasures of her fortunate namesake she exclaimed in admiration and
delight, and quite forgot for the time that she had
run away from home to visit a Tory's house, and that

Kathy, her dearest friend, was soon to sail away to a far-off island.

The broad window-seat was a very pleasant place on that warm June morning. There was a cool little breeze stirring among the branches of the trees near the open windows; and as Kathy carefully lifted the doll's dainty gowns and Annette tried them on her English namesake it was no wonder that she was conscious only of delight.

"Sir Guy sent me word that he would come and call on 'Miss Carleton,' so, you see, he expected me to name the doll for him," said Kathy, as if wishing to explain to Annette her reason for giving Annette's namesake the name of an English officer. "And of course I wanted to," she added quickly.

"Of course," Annette responded, remembering that, after all, the great General had been kind to wish to give pleasure to Kathy.

"Now you must see all my treasures," declared Kathy. "Oh, Annette, I have always wished and wished that you would spend a day with me, and now that you are really here it seems too good to be true."

Annette nodded happily, as she watched Kathy open the door of a cupboard and take out a small box of polished white wood.

"This is my work-box," said Kathy, placing it in Annette's lap. "My Grandmother Down sent it to me from London."

The box had a lock and key of gold; as Annette carefully opened it her face was reflected in a small oval mirror set in the cover. In the box was a gold thimble, a gold-mounted ivory bodkin, and an emery-ball shaped like a strawberry. There were spools of cotton and silk thread, and three pairs of scissors; and, carefully wrapped in a square of white silk, was a beaded purse that Kathy had begun.

"This is the pattern," said Kathy, showing Annette a square of paper on which was stamped a red rose with green leaves.

"The rose is to be all of shaded red beads, and the leaves of shaded greed beads," Kathy explained, "and on the other side is to be the initial of the name of the person I am making it for."

Annette did not ask for whom the purse was intended, but she felt quite sure that it must be for Sir Guy.

"Do you not want to work one of the tiny leaves, Annette?" questioned Kathy. "I will show you just the beads to select." But Annette shook her head.

"No, Kathy," she said soberly, thinking to herself that to set a stitch for an enemy of America would be disloyal.

The morning hours passed very quickly, and when a bell rang in the lower hall and Kathy exclaimed: "Why, that is the bell for dinner!" Annette could hardly believe it possible.

At the sound of the bell Kathy sprang up and clasping Annette's hand said: "Just think, Annette, this is the first time you have ever spent the day with me. And we are to have dinner all by ourselves. I do hope Phyllis has everything you like best;" and smiling happily the two little friends ran down-stairs to the big dining-room, where Phyllis had spread a round table for their dinner near the open windows.

For a moment Annette looked at the table wonderingly. It seemed to the little girl to be covered with a silvery light. The damask table-cloth shone, the lustre plates and cups reflected the light from the windows, and the covered dishes of silver shone clearly. In the centre of the table was a crystal dish filled with white roses. It was no wonder that Annette thought she had never before seen so lovely a table.

"Oh, Kathy! It is beautiful!" she exclaimed, as she took her seat opposite her young hostess.

Phyllis smiled delightedly. She had tried her best to please her young mistress. "Yo' jes' wait 'til yo' tastes de fine duck I'se cooked for yo'," she said, lifting the cover of one of the silver dishes; "an' dar is creamed pertaters, Missie Kathy; an' some fine lettis, yas'm; an' some little green peas. An' jes' look at dis jelly, an' har's some hot biscuit. Yas'm," and Phyllis served the delicious food, with approving nods and smiles as Kathy and Annette both declared that it was a beautiful dinner.

IT WAS A MERRY DINNER

"An' yo' jes' waits 'til yo' sees de cherry pie dat's a-comin'," said the delighted negress as she turned toward the kitchen.

"Oh, I meant to bring 'Annette Carleton' down to dinner!" Kathy exclaimed. "I will run up-stairs and fetch her, if you will excuse me, Annette?"

"Yes, indeed," was the quick response, and in a moment Kathy was back with the new doll, which she seated at the side of the table.

It was a merry dinner for the two little friends, and after Phyllis had brought in the cherry pie she returned to the kitchen well pleased with the result of her efforts to please "Missie Kathy."

"De pore chile don' hab no playmates in dis town, an' I'se right glad dat dis yere li'l' Vincen' gal is a vis-it'n' her," thought Phyllis, who had often been hurt and angry at the snubs and unfriendliness that Katherine had experienced from the American chil-dren, many of whom thought it a fine thing to be rude and uncivil to Kathy because her father was known to be a Tory, and friendly with the British officers. Annette alone among Kathy's acquain-tances had openly defended Kathy, and declared that the little girl was not to be blamed for her father's opinions. And it was this very thought that had sent Annette hurrying to her friend without waiting to ask permission.

Kathy and Annette had just finished dinner when a loud rapping at the front door made them look questioningly at each other. "I wonder who it can be," said Kathy in low tones, as she heard Phyllis hurrying through the hall. A moment later the colored girl appeared in the doorway. Phyllis's eyes were round and she was evidently greatly impressed by the importance of the visitor whom she had to announce.

"Massa Lord Sir Guy Carleton has arrived in de drawer-in'-room, Missie Kathy. An' he says he w'ud be please ter see yo'."

"Oh! Is he not kind to really ask for me?" exclaimed Kathy, smiling with delight, as if a visit from Sir Guy was the most wonderful thing that could happen, and jumping up from her chair, ready to start to welcome her visitor.

Annette had also sprung to her feet, but she was not smiling. There was a flush on her cheeks, and she looked at Kathy pleadingly.

"You won't see him, will you, Kathy?" she urged. "I would do anything you asked me to, this last day," she added. Before either of the girls could say another word a pleasant voice sounded from the open door, and Annette looked up to see a tall man in a fine scarlet coat, embroidered waistcoat and powdered wig smiling graciously at the two surprised little girls, and heard him say:

"Pardon me, Miss Katherine, for interrupting you when you have company," and Sir Guy bowed to Annette, "but I was passing and could not refrain from calling to ask after Miss Carleton, who, I am pleased to see, is lunching with you," and Sir Guy bowed to the doll as if she were really a fine lady.

"Thank you very much, Sir Guy. I am honored by your visit," responded Kathy, making her best curtsey. "And this is my friend, Annette Vincent," she continued.

"I am happy to meet Miss Annette Vincent," said Sir Guy, smiling at the solemn, dark-eyed little girl who made no response but turned and ran from the room.

For a moment Kathy was tempted to run after her. She felt hurt and shamed by Annette's behavior, and almost sorry that Sir Guy had appeared.

But the English General did not seem to notice Annette's departure. His glance had turned to the table and he was looking at the half of the cherry pie with approving eyes.

"Will you not taste of the cherry pie, Sir Guy?" Kathy asked eagerly. "It is one of Phyllis's best."

"Thank you, my dear. I will indeed," be replied, laying his cocked hat and gold-mounted whip on a side table and smilingly seating himself beside "Miss Carleton" while Phyllis hastened to provide him with napkin, knife and fork, and to help him to a generous piece of the cherry pie.

"Jes' a minit, Massa Lord Sir Guy, an' I'll fetch yo' a fine cup ob coffee," said Phyllis, hurrying off to the kitchen, to reappear before Sir Guy had finished the pastry with a steaming cup that the General declared excellent.

"I am indeed sorry that my mother is not at home," said Kathy, as Sir Guy rose from the table declaring that he had never tasted a better pie.

"I will do myself the pleasure of calling again," responded the visitor; and even Betty Mason could not have felt more a grown-up young lady than did Kathy as she made her prettiest curtsey, and thanked the General for the honor of his visit, for she had been carefully taught the rules of good manners.

"I hope your little friend will pardon me for frightening her away," said Sir Guy, as Kathy walked beside him to the front door.

At the door there was another ceremonious leave-taking, and Kathy, curtseying and smiling, stood in the doorway as Sir Guy mounted his fine black horse and rode off toward Broadway. The moment he was out of sight she ran back to the dining-room calling: "Annette! Annette!" but there was no response. Kathy hurried to the kitchen, but Phyllis had not seen the little girl.

"She must be up-stairs," Kathy decided, and hurried to her chamber, but Annette was not there.

"We must find her, Phyllis. You see, Annette thinks Sir Guy is an enemy to America, and so she would not speak to him, and ran out of the room," Kathy explained to the puzzled servant.

"My lan'! Dat's poor manners, Missie Kathy! 'Twan' no way fer a white lady to act," and grumbling over Annette's rudeness toward Sir Guy

Carleton, Phyllis followed her young mistress from room to room until at last Kathy was willing to acknowledge that Annette was not in the house.

"She put off fer home, Missie, dat's w'at she did," said Phyllis, and Kathy concluded Phyllis must be right, although Annette's hat was in Kathy's room.

It was a disappointing end to the visit that Kathy had hoped would be one of delight. She owned to herself that she wished Sir Guy Carleton had postponed his visit.

"Perhaps I will never see Annette again," she thought unhappily, as she lifted "Miss Annette Carleton" from her seat at the table and carried her up-stairs.

Phyllis went back to the kitchen. "I reckon dar's a tempes' comin'," she thought, as the branches of the elm tree near the kitchen windows swayed back and forth.

"An' dar ain' a breef of wind neither," she added, as she stepped to the door and looked out. "Lan'! I hope dar ain' no wile an'mal a-crouchin' in dat air tree," and Phyllis peered up anxiously into the branches that now only swayed quietly, and then turned back to her work thinking of the fine General's compliment to her cherry pie, and quite forgetting all about Annette, who at that very moment was crouching among the leafy branches of the big elm, wondering how she could escape from her uncomfortable perch without being discovered.

CHAPTER VI

IT was nearly noon before Mrs. Vincent discovered that her little daughter was missing. Annette often played about the garden for hours at a time, and as no one had seen the little girl enter or leave the house her mother believed her to be happily occupied under the big oak tree near the river, and just before the midday meal was served she walked down the box-bordered path to tell Annette that it was time to come in.

Mrs. Vincent did not feel at all anxious when she did not find Annette in the garden. "She has run up to her room to smooth her hair and make ready for dinner," she concluded, and on returning to the house called her little daughter's name, quite sure that Annette would come running into the dining-room. So she took her own seat at the table, and when Annette did not appear Lottie was sent to call her.

"Where can the child be?" she exclaimed, when Lottie declared that Annette was not in the house or garden. So at the very time when Kathy and Phyllis were searching for the missing visitor, Annette's mother and Lottie were anxiously looking for some trace of her in the Cherry Street house and garden.

"I wonder if John has taken Annette for a sail?" thought Mrs. Vincent, as she stood looking out on the quiet river. She finally decided that this was the explanation of the little girl's absence.

"Probably John intended to bring her back before dinner-time, but did not have a fair wind," she said to Lottie on returning to the house; "but Annette should not have gone without asking permission."

Lottie agreed that the little girl was doubtless on the *Fleetwing*, and would soon come running up the garden path eager for her dinner. "I'll jes' save dat col' custard an' some ob dem slices ob chicken fer her," decided the good-natured colored girl, as she cleared away the dinner table, and for a time neither Mrs. Vincent nor Lottie was disturbed by Annette's disappearance. But when the clock struck four and there was no sign of the little girl Mrs. Vincent became anxious, and sent Lottie to the house of Delia Davidson to ask if Delia had seen the missing girl; and when Mr. Vincent returned home at five o'clock from his office on Broad Street and was told that Annette had not been seen since early morning, he was seriously alarmed.

"John would not take Annette for a day's excursion without our knowledge," he declared, "and beside that fact, the lad was in my office not an hour ago, and said nothing of having been in his boat. No;

Annette must have left the house without permission. Perhaps Lottie will find her with Delia and bring her home."

But Lottie returned saying that Delia had not seen Annette.

"I reckon she gone to see de li'l' Tory gal dat she like so much," suggested Lottie.

"But I have never given her permission to go to Mr. Down's house," said Mrs. Vincent. "Kathy sometimes comes here, and is a well-behaved child, but I have never allowed Annette to return her visits."

"Yas'm, an' mebbe dat's why Missie Annette staht off widout askin'," suggested Lottie, as she went back to the kitchen.

"I had better go to Nassau Street and inquire," said Mr. Vincent, "although I like not to be seen on the Tory's porch. 'Tis said he means soon to take all his fine goods from the city."

"I think Lottie may be right," said Mrs. Vincent. "Annette, this very morning, received a note from Kathy."

At hearing this Mr. Vincent hesitated no longer, but hurried off to the fine Down mansion on Nassau Street, where he arrived just in time to encounter the British Adjutant-General De Lancey leaving the house in company with Mr. Down.

Mr. Down said that Annette was not there. "My little daughter is alone in the house with only the colored servant to keep her company, as her mother has not returned from a day's visit," he replied in response to Mr. Vincent's inquiries. Kathy had not mentioned Annette's visit and sudden flight to her father, so Mr. Down had no knowledge that the little girl had been in his home that day; and Mr. Vincent turned away more anxious than ever. He began to fear that Annette might have fallen into the river at the foot of the garden.

In the meantime the missing girl had been having a very uncomfortable afternoon. When she ran from the dining-room to avoid speaking to Sir Guy Carleton Annette had meant only to keep out of the way until Kathy's visitor had left the house. She ran through the kitchen to the narrow garden space behind the house, and looked about for a hiding-place. A low-growing branch of the big elm came within reach of the porch steps and Annette found she could easily reach it and draw herself up among the thickly growing leaves, and in a moment she had climbed to a perch on the strong branch where, by clasping another limb of the tree, she was well concealed.

"I won't have to stay here but a few minutes before the fine General will ride away," she thought, knowing that she would hear the sound of his horse's hoofs on the cobblestones.

But Annette had forgotten Phyllis, who, returning to the kitchen before the General's departure, came out on the porch just as the little girl had decided it was safe for her to descend; and Annette did not want the colored servant to see her scrambling down, like a frightened squirrel, from her hiding-place; and when Kathy and Phyllis began to search for her and call her name Annette began to wish that she had not run from the dining-room, and to realize that she had behaved in a rude and unseemly manner, and this made her ashamed to face Kathy.

"I will wait until they stop trying to find me, and then I will go home," Annette decided.

It soon became a difficult matter for her to keep her perch on the limb of the tree, and she decided to climb a little higher where she could sit on a limb with her back against the trunk of the tree, and it was this scrambling among the branches that had alarmed Phyllis when she stepped out on the porch.

Annette found the new place much more comfortable. She was now on the level of the windows of Katherine's chamber, and by pushing a bough of the tree a little to one side she could look in and see her hat lying on the bed, and "Miss Annette Carleton" again established in the silk-covered armchair.

It seemed a long time to Annette before Kathy and Phyllis gave up searching for her. Then she heard the sound of arriving visitors, and looking down saw that Phyllis had established herself in a rocking-chair on the porch where a negro girl from a neighboring house soon joined her, and Phyllis promptly began to describe the strange behavior of "dat li'l' 'Merican gal w'at was a-visitin' my li'l' Missie Kathy."

Annette could feel her face flush angrily as she heard Phyllis declare: "Dat Vincen' gal act like she nebber been taught no manners, Sukey! W'y, she nebber so much as look at Lord Sir Guy; an' she rush out ob de dinin'-room like she was a sabage! Lan'! Dar sho' am sum animal a-lurkin' in dat tree!" concluded Phyllis, looking anxiously up as Annette moved about on the swaying bough.

It was no wonder, after hearing this account of her behavior, that Annette had no wish to be discovered by any member of the Down household. She was sure that Kathy's mother and father had returned home and that Kathy had told them of Annette's rudeness. As she thought it over the little girl realized that it had not been fair to Kathy to treat Kathy's visitor in such a manner.

"Sir Guy will only think all little American girls ill-mannered, and probably Kathy will never want to see me again," thought the unhappy child, who now wished with all her heart that she had not run away from home that morning.

Phyllis and her friend did not move from the porch until late in the afternoon, and even then Phyllis was busy near the kitchen windows so that Annette realized she must think of some other way of escaping from her leafy prison.

"I believe I could get into Kathy's room," she thought, noticing that the stout branch of the big tree touched the house.

The more Annettee thought of this way of escape the more possible it seemed. If she could reach Kathy's room she could put on her hat, and then perhaps creep down the stairs and reach the street without being seen; and she resolved to make the attempt.

It was a perilous adventure, for she must walk along the swaying bough for several feet without anything to hold for support, and a single misstep or lack of balance would cause her to fall crashing down into the yard below.

But Annette was not conscious of any fear as she rose carefully to her feet. Her whole mind was fixed on reaching Kathy's chamber; and she stepped out cautiously, balancing herself so carefully that the limb of the tree hardly moved until her hands clasped the sill of the window when, for brief moment, she swung clear of the tree. But she had a secure hold and was able to pull herself over the window-sill on to the broad seat where for a few moments she lay motionless, half expecting to hear Kathy exclaim or cry out at her appearance. But as she sat up and looked about the room there was no sign of Kathy, and in a moment Annette had tiptoed across the room and tied on her straw hat. She then peered out into the shadowy upper hall. There was no one to be seen, and no sound of voices or steps; so Annette ventured out and went softly down the stairs and through the open door and reached Nassau Street where little groups of people were moving along the sidewalks.

She began to feel very tired, and could not race along toward home as she wished to do. It was the beginning of the long June twilight, and the streets were already shadowed by the approaching darkness. As the little girl walked slowly along St. George's Square she heard the steady ring of a bell, and saw a man approaching who called out:

"Child lost! Little girl missing! Brown eyes, and brown hair. Ten years old! Child lost!"

After every word the man rang the bell as loudly as possible. He passed close to Annette, who stood for a moment looking after him with puzzled eyes.

"I do believe it's I!" she whispered to herself, and resolved to quicken her pace and reach home as soon as possible; at that very moment she felt a firm clasp on her arm and looked up to find her Cousin John standing beside her.

CHAPTER VII

A PEACE TREATY

"I was just going home, John! Is it I that's lost?" asked Annette, as John, still holding his cousin firmly by the hand, hurried her along the street, stopping to call the Crier and tell him that the lost girl had been discovered.

The cousins had turned into Cherry Street before John spoke to the little girl.

"Where have you been?" he asked sharply.

"I have been to Kathy Down's, and Sir Guy Carleton came, and—" Annette would have told the whole story of flying from the Downs' dining-room without speaking to the British General, and of climbing the tree, but John interrupted her angrily:

"Visiting a Tory, and talking with the enemies of your country, and thinking nothing of anyone but yourself," he said. "Your mother feared you must have fallen into the river, and is sadly anxious about you. And your father and neighbors are searching the town for you," and John gave his cousin's arm an impatient shake as if to express his disapproval.

Annette was too tired and unhappy to defend herself. The day with Kathy, that the little friends had expected to be full of delight, a day that they would always joyfully remember, had been a most wretched disappointment. It was difficult for Annette to keep back the tears, and when her mother came running down the street to meet them and John let go his clasp on her arm Annette fled toward her mother and sobbed out: "Mother! Mother! I didn't mean to run away," at which John exclaimed:

"A likely story," and turned away to find Annette's father and tell him that the little girl was safe at home.

Mrs. Vincent led the tired little girl indoors, bathed the tear-stained face, and told Lottie to bring a tray with Annette's supper to her chamber, and there in the fragrant June twilight by the open window, with her mother's arm about her, Annette told the story of the day.

"Nobody is fair to Kathy, Mother," she pleaded. "That is why I started off to see her. None of the girls go to see her, and she never, never, says a disloyal word about America; but all the grown-ups think she is a Tory. And, Mother, when you seemed pleased that she could not go with me to Greenwich Village, it did seem as if I must see Kathy."

"I wish you had told me, dear, instead of running off without a word; I would have sent Lottie to ask Kathy to come and see you," responded Mrs. Vincent.

"But, Mother, Kathy could not come. You See, she has been here several times, and now her mother will not permit her to come unless I visit Kathy. Oh, Mother, I had to go," Annette declared earnestly, and went on to tell of the doll, and of the visit of the British General, her own rude behavior, and the long hours in the elm tree. But she did not betray Kathy's secret of the speedy departure of the Downs from New York.

"Oh! My dear girl, I am indeed to blame that you should do such a thing," exclaimed Mrs. Vincent, as Annette told of running from the dining-room.

"You, Mother! You! Why, you would not be rude to anyone; not even to the King of England, who sent the soldiers here," declared Annette.

"Then how is it that my own little daughter could forget that she was a guest, and that the first duty of a guest is to think of her hostess's feelings, and to treat other visitors with courtesy? Surely I am to blame," Mrs. Vincent insisted; for she never punished Annette, knowing that a wrong act surely brings its own punishment; but this was always carefully explained to the little girl.

"No, Mother! I did know better than to be rude, but I did not stop to think," said Annette.

Before Annette went to sleep that night she had made a firm resolve: she would, with her mother's permission, go to Kathy's home the next morning and ask Kathy to pardon her impoliteness; besides this she would do something much more difficult: she would call on Sir Guy Carleton himself and beg his pardon for her discourtesy. Comforted by this resolve Annette slept soundly and awoke next morning hoping her mother would give her consent for her to go to Mr. Down's at an early hour.

"Yes, my dear. I was sure you would wish to ask Kathys' pardon, and Lottie can go with you to Mr. Down's door. Ask to see Kathy, tell her why you have come, and then come straight home," said Mrs. Vincent, in response to Annette's request.

"But I want to ask pardon of Sir Guy," Annette continued. "Phyllis said the General would think all little American girls were ill-mannered, but if I tell him I am sorry perhaps he will not think that."

For a moment Mrs. Vincent was silent. Americans living in New York during the British occupation had been badly treated, and to permit her little girl to go to the house of Sir Guy to ask his pardon was not an easy decision for Mrs. Vincent to reach, nevertheless she realized that it would be a lesson Annette would never forget, and she replied that Sir Guy was sure to think more highly of all little American girls if Annette owned her fault.

"And you shall wear your checked silk dress, and your blue hat, and carry the fine white parasol that Grandmother Vincent gave you," said Mrs. Vincent; "and be sure and make your best curtsey to the British General, that he may know little American girls can be well-mannered."

"Indeed I will, Mother," responded the little girl, beginning to think her errand might not be so difficult after all.

It was nine o'clock when Annette and Lottie set forth for Nassau Street. Lottie wore a freshly starched dress of brown cotton, and with her big white apron and carefully twisted blue turban she felt herself quite ready to face the fine servants of the Tory houses, and she smiled delightedly as they started down Cherry Street, well pleased with her morning's duty of escorting her young mistress.

But Annette's face was very serious. Not even the pretty white parasol or wearing her silk mitts and best dress could make the little girl entirely forget that she must face Sir Guy Carleton and ask him to pardon her for her rude behavior. Now and then she sighed deeply, at which Lottie would look anxiously down at the little figure beside her and wonder if her little mistress was ill.

As they approached the Down house the big front door opened and Mrs. Down stepped out, followed by Kathy, and for a moment Annette hesitated. She had said to herself that she would not mind telling Kathy that she was sorry for running out of the dining-room, but to say it before Kathy's mother was a very different and much more difficult undertaking.

"Oh, Annette! I am so glad to see you. Why did you run away yesterday?" exclaimed Kathy, hurrying to meet her friend and looking admiringly at Annette's fine apparel. Mrs. Down also greeted the little girl cordially, as Annette curtseyed deeply.

"If you please, I must not come in," she said in response to Kathy's invitation. "I came to tell you, Kathy, that I am indeed sorry for my behavior yesterday, and to ask you to pardon me." Annette did not raise her eyes as she spoke; her face flushed and her voice trembled. She thought to herself that in the future she would never, never forget to be polite, no matter what might happen, but she had hardly finished her plea when Katherine's arms were about her neck and she heard Kathy say:

"Oh, Annette, I did not mind for myself. It was only because Sir Guy is so kind to me."

"What is all this?" inquired Mrs. Down, becoming puzzled at the mention of the name of the British General, and Annette realized that Kathy had not told her mother of her friend's sudden disappearance.

"If you please, Mrs. Down, I ran out of the dining-room yesterday when Sir Guy came in," said Annette, "and I came this morning to ask Kathy's pardon."

"I should think so, indeed," declared Mrs. Down, looking at Annette with evident disapproval. "Come, Katherine, we will not detain your visitor any longer," and taking Kathy by the the hand she drew her away from Annette and started toward the street.

"Good-bye, dear Annette," Kathy called back, but Annette made no response.

"Don' yo' min', Missie," comforted Lottie. "Dey ain' no 'count. I hears dat Governor Clinton an' Massa Washington are gwine ter drive dese Tories right outer New Yo'k mos' any time now. Don' yo' min' 'em, honey."

But Annette was not listening to the good-natured darkey's words. If Mrs. Down thought her rudeness so unforgivable, what would the British General say to her? For a moment Annette was tempted to go home without even trying to see Sir Guy.

"Oh, dear!" she exclaimed aloud, and stood looking after Kathy, then a little smile crept over her face; she was thinking to herself that Kathy was sure to hear of her visit to Sir Guy, and that after hearing it she would be sure to believe that Annette was really sorry. "Kathy always understands," thought the little girl as she and Lottie turned into Wall Street, where they met a number of British officers out for a morning stroll.

"My lan', Missie Kathy, be yo' a-callin' on de General hisse'f?" asked the delighted Lottie as Annette stopped in front of the fine mansion occupied by Sir Guy Carleton. The little girl did not have time to reply before a tall soldier, standing at the entrance, asked her errand.

"If you please, I am Miss Annette Vincent, and I wish to see Sir Guy Carleton," Annette responded, her voice trembling a little.

The soldier smiled down at the General's little visitor as he replied:

"Will Miss Vincent kindly step into the reception-room while I inform Sir Guy?" and Annette followed him into a large room at the right of the front door, and seated herself on the edge of a chair facing the door. Lottie waited in the hall, now and then peering into the reception-room to make sure that her young mistress was quite safe.

It seemed a long time to Annette before the tall soldier returned and said that she was to follow him up the broad staircase.

Lottie started to follow them, but the soldier waved her back. "Your young mistress will be back in a brief time," he said.

"Miss Annette Vincent, to call on Sir Guy," said the soldier to a servant in fine livery, who stood at the top of the staircase, and who quickly opened a door behind him, saying, "Miss Annette Vincent." The door closed behind her, and Annette found herself facing the British General, who rose from his desk at the further end of the long room and bowed to his visitor.

Annette curtseyed low, then advanced a few steps and curtseyed again.

Sir Guy smiled approvingly at the brown-eyed little girl in her dainty summer dress. He did not recognize this attractive little lady as the rude girl who had fled yesterday at his entrance to the Downs' dining-room.

For a moment Annette was sure that she was not going to be able to speak. All the long way from Cherry Street she had repeated over and over to herself just what she would say to Sir Guy Carleton, and now she felt choked and as if she had no voice. It was evident that Sir Guy was puzzled as he said politely:

"Will you not sit down, and perhaps there is some favor you wish to ask of me?"

"If you please, sir, I am Kathy Down's friend, and I ran from the dining-room when you came to see her yesterday," faltered the little girl.

"Ah-h! Yes. You are, I suppose, one of the little rebels of New York," replied Sir Guy, his smile disappearing as he spoke.

"I have come to ask you to pardon my rudeness, Sir Guy. I am sure no other little American girl would behave in so ill-mannered a fashion as I did yesterday," continued Annette earnestly, regaining her courage and looking up at the tall General as if pleading for his good opinion of the manners of American children.

"Perhaps you are not a rebel after all," responded Sir Guy. "Miss Kathy is the daughter of a faithful Loyalist, and if you are her friend, why you must be my friend also, and I am quite sure you meant no rudeness in running away from me yesterday. I am rather glad you did, since it has brought you to see me this morning," and Sir Guy made a very fine bow to his little visitor.

"Thank you, sir," said Annette. "But, if you please, I am a little American girl."

"Well, we will shake hands, Miss America, for after this, you know, England and America are to be friends. Very soon my soldiers will return to their homes, and I to mine. I would like to leave one friend behind me. Will not you be that friend?" and Sir Guy looked kindly down at the sober-faced little girl who stood before him.

Annette looked up questioningly. How kind and honest this Englishman seemed, she thought wonderingly.

"You will not fight against America's rights again, will you?" she questioned eagerly.

"Not if I can help it," he answered.

"Then I will always be your friend," Annette declared, and the great British commander and the little American girl clasped hands as if they were forever settling the friendship between England and America.

CHAPTER VIII

A HAPPY MEETING

ANNETTE was very quiet all the way home that morning, but she was much happier than when she had run through the same streets the previous day on her runaway visit to Kathy Down. She was eager to reach home and tell her mother of Sir Guy's promise not to again fight against America's rights, unless compelled to do so, and she ran into the Cherry Street house calling "Mother! Mother!" and did not stop to take off her best hat or lay aside the pretty white parasol before beginning her story.

Mrs. Vincent had been at work in the garden, and came up on the cool porch to listen to her little daughter's description of meeting Kathy and Mrs. Down, and of her visit to the British General.

"Sir Guy was pleased to see me, truly he was, Mother, dear; and he asked me to be his friend, and I promised. Mother, what are America's 'rights'? I know that is what the war was about, but when I asked Sir Guy to promise not to fight against our 'rights' again, why, all at once I realized I did not know what America's rights are. I thought about it all the way home," and Annette looked at her mother questioningly.

"Why, my dear child! Have you not often heard your father read America's 'Declaration of Independence'? We must ask him to read it this evening. And very soon, I am sure, you will hear General Washington himself read it here in New York."

But Annette was still looking at her mother as if waiting for an answer, and with a little laugh Mrs. Vincent continued: "Well, Annette, the war of the American Revolution was fought because the rulers of England taxed us unfairly for their own profit, without caring for the hardships such taxation inflicted on Americans; without permitting us even to help make the laws under which we must live. Do you understand, dear?"

Annette nodded thoughtfully. "I guess so," she responded, a little doubtfully. "They wanted to tell us what we must do, whether it was right or not."

"Exactly, and because they were selfish and unfair they failed, and now Americans have established their own government, and this has become a free country, governed by its own citizens, and Sir Guy Carleton and all his soldiers must leave this city," said Mrs. Vincent. "Now, my dear, run up-stairs and put your parasol and mitts carefully away, change your dress and help me shell peas for dinner," and Annette hastened to obey.

As she slipped on her simple gingham dress she remembered that she was to go to Greenwich Village the next day, and wished that Kathy might go also, and this reminded her of Kathy's secret.

"Oh, what will I do when Kathy has really left New York and I can never see her again?" she thought sadly, as she went slowly down the stairs to the back porch.

"After dinner we must pack the things you will need for your visit to Grandma's," said Mrs. Vincent. "Your father plans to drive you over early in the morning before the heat of the day. Do you not want to ask Delia or Betty to go with you?"

Annette shook her head. "No, if Kathy cannot go I do not want anyone," she declared, with such a sober face that Mrs. Vincent felt troubled.

"Your Grandmother Vincent thought you would enjoy your visit more if you had a friend with you. You know there are no children near for you to play with," she said.

But Annette made no reply. She thought to herself that her mother did not seem to realize that she was nearly eleven years old, and that she and Grandma were good friends and companions. Besides, thought Annette, there was Kathy's secret to think over.

"Oh, dear! I wish—" she exclaimed suddenly, and then looked up, half frightened as she realized that she had been about to say that she wished Kathy Down was not going to Bermuda! But apparently her mother had not noticed her exclamation, and nothing more was said in regard to the visit to Greenwich

Village. But all that afternoon Annette could think only of Kathy; that perhaps she might never again see the playmate she liked so well. For had not Kathy said that they might sail for that far-off island before Annette returned from her visit to Grandma Vincent? Annette wandered about the garden and up to her own chamber, then to the porch where her mother was busy sewing, until her mother began to wonder at her little daughter's uneasiness.

"Annette, where is your sewing? Did I not set you a stint early in the week? You were to finish the aprons for Lottie, and I have not yet seen you set a stitch," she said.

"Oh, Mother, so much has happened," Annette replied. "May I not take the aprons with me and finish them at Grandma's? I shall like to sit with her and sew."

Mrs. Vincent agreed to this suggestion, for she realized that it had been an eventful week for the little girl. Annette went to bed early, and was awake in good season the next morning. Robins and songsparrows were singing in the tall elms, or fluttering down to the garden for their morning rations; Lottie was singing about her work in the kitchen, and a cool little breeze came up from the river. The sorrel horse was harnessed to the comfortable chaise and stood waiting for its passengers as Annette finished her breakfast and came running to the front porch to watch her father stow the small leather trunk that held her pretty summer dresses under the broad seat of the chaise. Then Mrs. Vincent kissed the little girl good-bye, her father lifted her into the chaise and they drove off, stopping at the street corner to turn and wave to Annette's mother, who stood on the steps looking after them.

For the time Annette had forgotten about Kathy's departure. The morning was cool and pleasant, she was wearing her white muslin dress and her open-work stockings; the sorrel horse trotted along at a good pace; her father was singing John's favorite song: "Bright Castabella," and Annette could think only of the pleasant ride to Greenwich Village, and how glad Grandma would be to see them.

The road to Greenwich was a popular drive for the British officers, and early though it was, Annette and her father soon met a party of red-coats on horse-back galloping back to town after a morning ride.

Annette leaned from the chaise to watch them dash past, and instantly one of the party drew rein, lifted his hat in salute to the little girl and was out of sight in an instant.

"Father! Father! Did you see Sir Guy Carleton bow to me?" exclaimed the little girl, clasping her father's arm with both hands. "And did I tell you that he is my friend?" and she looked up eagerly into her father's face.

"He is Kathy Down's friend too. He gave her a most beautiful doll from Paris," she added.

Before Mr. Vincent could respond Annette was nearly out of the chaise in her impetuous effort to attract the notice of another little girl seated beside a stout man in a fine chaise that was now just passing the Vincents.

"Kathy! Kathy Down!" called Annette, and Kathy instantly called back:

"Annette! Annette!" adding in the same breath, "Oh, stop the horse, Father! Stop him," and Mr. Down instantly complied. Mr. Vincent also drew rein, bringing the two carriages side by side so that the two little girls were near enough to each other to clasp hands, while the two fathers saluted each other gravely.

"Oh, Kathy, I am so glad to see you!" Annette exclaimed. "I am just starting for my visit to Grandma's."

"My father and I have just taken Mother to Richmond Hill," responded Kathy.

"I do wish you could go with me to Greenwich Village. May not Kathy go with me, Mr. Down? There is plenty of room for her in the chaise," and Annette moved closer to her father to show that there was indeed room for another passenger.

"May I not go, Father?" pleaded Kathy, "and when you come for Mother this evening you can fetch me home."

Mr. Down smiled good-naturedly. He was well pleased that Kathy should not be left alone with the colored servants in the big Nassau Street house, so he said: "Why, if your little friend really wishes your company, and if you, sir," with a polite bow to Mr. Vincent, "are willing, I have no objection."

"I shall be glad to have Miss Kathy for a passenger," replied Mr. Vincent, for, although he believed Mr. Down to have been an enemy to America's liberties, he remembered that the war was over and that the Americans had triumphed and could afford to treat their recent foes with courtesy; besides that he knew that it would give Annette great delight to have Kathy as her companion, and in a moment Kathy was seated beside her friend, Mr. Down had driven on toward the city, and Annette's wish had come true. Kathy was going with her to Greenwich Village.

The two little friends chattered gaily, and now and then exchanged glances of radiant happiness.

"This shall be our happiest day to remember," Annette whispered, as Mr. Vincent turned into the well-shaded driveway leading to his mother's home.

The house stood on a rise of ground that fell away in the rear in a gentle slope to the water side. There was a broad veranda across the back commanding a fine view down the harbor. In front there was a flower garden, through which the drive led to the front door.

As they drew near the house a small white dog rushed around the corner, barking so savagely that he nearly fell over at every bark.

"Here, here, Lion!" called Mr. Vincent, laughingly, and at the sound of a familiar voice the dog's fierce barks ceased and he came running to the side of the chaise ready to welcome the newcomers.

"Lion's" bark brought Madame Vincent hurrying to the open door, and in a moment Annette was out of the chaise, saying, "Grandma, dear Grandma Vincent, I've come to stay a week and brought my dearest friend, Kathy Down," and then Kathy was smiling and curtseying as Madame Vincent made her little guests welcome, greeted her son, and then holding Annette by one hand and Kathy by the other, she led the way straight to the dining-room, where the table was spread with dishes heaped with fresh strawberries, a tall glass pitcher filled with cream and glasses of cool milk.

"I knew you would be ready for a second breakfast after your drive," said Grandma, smiling at her tall son, as they took their places at the table and an elderly negress brought in freshly baked muffins, broiled ham and coffee for Mr. Vincent.

"Lion" kept close to Annette, and when breakfast was over and the little girls went out on the back veranda facing the harbor he trotted after them, as if he felt responsible for their safety.

"We can go wherever we please, Kathy, Grandma said that we might, and when she wants us she will ring a bell," said Annette, "and if we go out to the stables we can see a colt."

"What is a 'colt'?" questioned Kathy, greatly to Annette's amusement, who was delighted to explain that a colt was a " baby horse," and as they followed the path leading to the stables Annette told her friend of a family of squirrels that lived in a hollow stump at the foot of the garden.

While the little girls, with the fat little white dog following them, wandered about the gardens Madame Vincent and her son were talking of Annette's new friend, Sir Guy Carleton, and his delay in removing the British troops from New York. "I am sure the Tories of the city are trying their best to keep him here," said Madame Vincent, "and I hear that Merchant Down means to move all his fine goods from the city. How does it happen that Annette chooses a Tory girl for her best friend?"

"Why, I think it is because the other girls treated Kathy Down unfairly," responded Annette's father. "You see, Annette is too good an American to believe in injustice, and Kathy is in no way to blame for her father's disloyalty. Then, too, Kathy is a pleasant and well-behaved child."

Mrs. Vincent nodded. "Well, I never doubted but that we should love our enemies; perhaps after all it is the way to conquer them, and I have no fault to find with Annette's little friend, but I fear New York will be in a sad state when it becomes an American city again."

"Governor Clinton and General Washington will soon set things straight," declared Mr. Vincent hopefully, "and it cannot be many weeks now before Sir Guy sails for home. Now I must say good-bye to Annette and return home," and with his mother beside him, Mr. Vincent started for the garden.

CHAPTER IX

AT THE FARM IN THE WOODS

AFTER Mr. Vincent had started for home his mother joined her little guests, and they walked together down the slope to the water's edge.

"There used to be an Indian village on this very spot," said Madame Vincent, "and it is probable that the Indians who came out in their canoes to Hendrik Hudson's ship, the *Half Moon*, and brought him vegetables and fruits set forth from this place."

Both Annette and Kathy remembered that it was Hendrik Hudson who in 1609 came sailing up the river that was afterwards named for him, and they looked about trying to imagine the wigwams of the Indians who had lived there before the Dutch and English settlers came.

"And this used to be called 'Farm in the Woods,' did it not, Grandma?" said Annette, and Madame Vincent nodded smilingly as she replied:

"Yes, and there is a Hendrik Hudson and his family and an Indian Chief living now on this very farm."

"Oh, Grandma Vincent!" exclaimed Annette, while Kathy's grey eyes opened wide in astonishment.

"Step very softly and I will show you where they live," said Madame Vincent, and she turned into a path leading along the shore, and the little girls followed her noiselessly. In a few moments they came to a big beech tree whose branches reached out over the water.

"Now stand very still and watch the lower branch," whispered Grandma, and almost before she had finished speaking there was a flash of blue wings and they saw a bird drop through the air into the water and in an instant dart back to its perch holding a fish in its bill.

"There he is, 'Indian Chief,' " declared Grandma Vincent, as eager and interested as were Annette and Kathy. "He has his nest in that tree, and he never goes very far away."

" 'Tis a kingfisher," said Annette.

"Mother calls it a halcyon," said Kathy.

"Yes, of course, but here he is 'Indian Chief,' because two hundred years ago little Indian girls may have watched these birds dive into these very waters," responded Grandma, "and now if we keep very quiet, Hendrik Hudson may bring his family to take a look at us."

As Madame Vincent spoke she picked up "Lion," who had kept close to Annette, and held him firmly, saying, "Quiet, Lion!"

Annette and Kathy smiled happily at each other. They were both thinking how wonderful it was to be together in this place where long ago little Indian girls had played, and where sailors from far-off lands had come to make a home. It was but a moment before they heard a little scrambling noise about the roots of the big tree, and then a grey furry head with bright, shining eyes peered out at them, looked sharply about, and then came boldly out quite near to Annette, showing himself to be a fat grey squirrel.

"Hendrik Hudson," whispered Grandma. Hendrik made a quick circle of the tree and disappeared, but the little girls had hardly time to miss him before he was back again, closely followed by two smaller squirrels. Then, quite as if they had been expecting visitors, the three furry grey squirrels perched themselves along the root of the tree and looked earnestly at the little girls.

"I usually bring them nuts or a bit of rock sugar," whispered Grandma. "Just reach in my bag, Annette, and you'll find some filberts."

So Annette put her hand in the embroidered silken bag that hung from Grandma's arm and in a moment the squirrels were darting here and there after the nuts that Annette threw about, while "Lion" moved uneasily in his mistress's arms.

"Now I must return to the house, my dears, and you can do whatever you please," said Grandma, as the squirrels fled off to store away the nuts for use on some stormy day, and " Lion" was permitted to again follow the little girls as they turned back toward the house, for Kathy had said to Madame Vincent, "I think we would like to go with you, if you please," greatly to Madame's delight and approval.

But as they reached the wide veranda Annette suddenly remembered that Kathy had not yet seen the family of ducks that lived on the shores of a tiny pond behind the stable, so the two little girls started off, while Grandma Vincent went indoors.

"Lion" followed the young visitors, and Kathy and Annette both laughed at the sober way in which the fat little white dog would look up at them whenever they turned to speak to him.

They passed the stable-yard where the long-legged brown colt stuck his nose over the fence and whinnied, as if asking them to stop and play with him, and Kathy laughed happily as she exclaimed:

"What do you suppose the colt's name is?"

"Perhaps it isn't named, and if it isn't I will ask Grandma to let us name it," Annette responded, adding quickly: "Oh, Kathy, isn't it splendid that we are way off here in Greenwich Village by ourselves?"

"Yes," Kathy agreed, "but I can only stay until sunset."

"Perhaps you can. Perhaps you can stay all the week," Annette rejoined hopefully, thinking to herself that she must try in some way to keep Kathy, and wondering if such a thing would be possible.

They visited the duck pond, and the gardener gave them some grain to feed the young ducklings and told

THEY VISITED THE DUCK POND

them that wild ducks, "bluebills," he called them, often came up near the shore at the foot of the garden.

"Is the colt named yet?" Annette asked, and the old gardener shook his head.

"I do not think the mistress has yet thought of a name for it. But you may be sure 'twill have a fine name when she does. Why, every animal on this place is named," he said smilingly.

"Let us hurry and ask Grandma," said Annette, and the two girls ran back toward the house, with "Lion" bouncing along behind them.

Madame Vincent was sitting on the veranda. "Dinner is waiting," she called, as the girls came running up the steps, and at the sound of her voice the elderly colored woman appeared in the open doorway, drew out a small square table and while Annette asked about the colt's name the table was spread with broiled chicken, jelly, baked potatoes and new peas; glasses were filled with milk and the little girls took their places on each side of Madame Vincent, while Marrilla hurried away for the hot muffins. The girls thought it a fine thing to have dinner in the open air and smiled happily at each other.

"Have you thought of a name good enough for so pretty a colt?" asked Grandma, looking at the eager young faces.

"I want Kathy to name it, if you please, Grandma," said Annette.

"Yes, indeed, so she shall," Grandma Vincent responded quickly, well pleased with her little grand-daughter's thoughtfulness. "And what name shall it be?" and she turned her friendly smile toward the little Tory girl.

Kathy smiled back radiantly. Annette had told her of the visit to Sir Guy, and Kathy thought to herself that Annette was sure to be pleased if she named the colt for her new friend. The little girl did not realize that to her kind hostess Sir Guy's name was a reminder of trouble, of war and sacrifice, so she said confidently: "Then I name the colt 'Sir Guy,'" and she looked smilingly toward Madame Vincent and Annette, quite sure of their approval.

For a moment there was silence. Even Annette realized Kathy's mistake, but when her grandmother said quietly: "Very well, my dear, that shall be the colt's name," Annette looked up gratefully, thinking how lovely Grandma always was, and loving her even more dearly for not letting Kathy even imagine that the name of the British General was a name she would be glad to forget.

"Would it not be splendid if Kathy could stay a week, Grandma?" suggested Annette, as they left the table.

"It would indeed. Perhaps, Kathy, your mother—" but before Madame Vincent could say another word Kathy exclaimed:

"Oh, I forgot! I forgot! My father did not know that my mother had forbidden me to come!" and the little girl stood looking at Annette with so unhappy an expression that both Annette and her grandmother were eager to comfort her.

"Your mother will be sure to understand that you did not mean to disobey, and as your father gave his permission for the day's visit, I am sure you need not be troubled," said Grandma, and Kathy grew more hopeful.

"It is not as if you planned to disobey," said Annette, and Kathy was comforted and smiled again. "Father always understands," she said gravely, and the little cloud that had threatened the day's sunshine disappeared.

"Would you not like to take some sugar to 'Sir Guy'?" suggested Grandma Vincent, giving each of the girls some bits of rock sugar, greatly to their delight, and they were off instantly to inform the brown colt that he now had a name.

"Let's climb to the top of the fence, then 'Sir Guy' can take the sugar from our hands," suggested Annette. Kathy promptly agreed, and in a moment they were perched on the upper rail, while the colt eagerly nibbled the lumps that each little girl cautiously held out to him. He seemed to enjoy having his head smoothed nearly as much as he did the sugar.

"It's too bad to keep 'Sir Guy' shut up in such a little yard," said Annette. "Let's open the gate and lead him about the garden. You can walk on one side and I'll hold on to his mane. I'm sure he'd like to walk about under the trees."

"Yes, indeed. Of course he would, and I think you are kind to think of it," said Kathy, scrambling down from the fence, closely followed by Annette, and in a moment they had lifted the bar that fastened the gate of the enclosure.

For a moment the colt stared at his new friends as if wondering just what was going to happen, then as the little girls came toward him he whinnied approvingly, thinking they were bringing him more sugar, and was quite ready to be led outside the yard. Then he halted, looked about as if he had discovered a new world, and in an instant he had leaped beyond the reach of Annette and Kathy and was racing across flower beds and box-bordered paths toward the shore, while "Lion," with frantic barks, ran wildly after him.

"Oh, Kathy, we must catch him! We must!" called Annette, and away they ran in pursuit. Now and then the colt would stop suddenly as if waiting for them, and then as they drew near he was off again.

When he was close to the shore the colt turned suddenly and leaped a low hedge into a field, and the girls had to search for an opening in the hedge to get through, and reached the field just in time to see "Sir Guy" spring over another hedge into a road.

After him they went, tearing their muslin dresses and scratching their hands, but thinking only of capturing the runaway. "Lion" had given up the chase and went panting back to rest on the cool veranda, but neither Annette nor Kathy thought about the fat little white dog as they ran along the rough road.

But the brown colt could run much faster than his pursuers, and when Kathy stumbled and fell and Annette stopped to help her friend to her feet, "Sir Guy" disappeared.

"I can't run another step," declared Kathy, as she hobbled along after her fall; "both my feet hurt and I'm tired."

"So am I," said Annette, "but I don't dare rest. You wait here, Kathy, under this tree and I'll run on 'til I catch the colt. I don't believe he will go much farther, and I'll lead him back here and by that time you will be rested, and we can get home before Grandma has missed us."

Kathy gratefully agreed to this plan. She leaned back against the wayside tree with a tired sigh, and Annette hurried on in the direction the colt had taken.

On and on plodded the tired little girl, but there was no sign of the missing "Sir Guy." A slow-moving brook crossed the road, and Annette stopped to take off her shoes and stockings and then, holding them in her hands, started to wade across the shallow little stream, but almost at the first step her foot slipped and down she splashed on her hands and knees. In a moment she had scrambled to her feet and made her way to the further bank.

"Oh, what will I do?" she whimpered, as she endeavored to wring the water from her skirts, and for the moment entirely forgot about the runaway colt.

CHAPTER X

THE BROWN COLT

GRANDMA VINCENT took her usual afternoon nap and returned to the veranda to find "Lion" curled up in a shady corner, apparently tired out. But she did not feel uneasy at the absence of her little visitors until Grimm, the old Scotch gardener, came hurrying across the garden.

"The brown colt is gone, ma'am!" he announced. "The gate has been opened, and I fear thieves have taken him."

In a moment Madame Vincent was hastening toward the stable-yard, closely followed by the anxious Grimm, who explained that while at work in a distant part of the farm he had heard "Lion" barking fiercely.

"But I thought 'twas some game with the lassies and paid no attention," he explained. Neither Madame Vincent nor the gardener connected Annette and Kathy with the disappearance of the colt, and Grimm began a careful search of the near-by fields for the missing animal, while his mistress walked about the garden, expecting every moment to hear Annette's voice or to come upon her little visitors. But as the long summer afternoon faded into twilight and the

104

girls did not appear, Mrs. Vincent returned to the house and rang the bell to summon them.

"They are playing somewhere along the shore," she explained to Marrilla, who did not like to keep supper waiting.

But when the girls failed to return, Grandma Vincent became anxious. Grimm had come back from his vain search after the colt, and now, with Madame Vincent and Marrilla went up and down the garden paths, through the stables, and searched the house for some trace of the missing girls. The stars of the summer night shone softly through the branches of the tall trees, the moon rose and silvered the waters where the kingfisher watched for his prey, and there was no trace or sign of what had befallen Annette and Kathy, and Mrs. Vincent had just decided that Grimm must start for Cherry Street to tell Annette's father of her disappearance when there came a loud knock at the front door and Marrilla hurried to answer it, and Madame Vincent heard a loud voice announce:

"I have come for Miss Katherine Down," and she hastened to the front hall to find an English soldier standing in the open door.

At the sight of Madame Vincent he quickly removed his cap and explained that Mr. Down had been prevented by business from coming after his daughter, and as he was riding in the direction of Greenwich Village, he had offered to call for the little girl. "Mrs. Down drove home with her friends in the afternoon," he added.

The soldier listened to the story of the strange disappearance of Annette and Kathy, and of the missing colt, with a puzzled expression; but as Madame Vincent finished her story, he said:

"Why, I believe the girls must have started off with the colt. Perhaps they thought they could ride it to the city."

This suggestion made Annette's grandmother very anxious indeed, but before she could speak, "Lion" began to bark loudly, there was a call from Grimm, and the brown colt appeared walking sedately up the driveway. In some way he had found his way safely back and was well pleased to be led to the stable-yard by the puzzled Grimm.

The soldier offered to ride along the highway and look for the lost children, and Madame Vincent was glad of his offer of assistance, and he was just mounting his horse when two shadowy little figures came slowly up the path and "Lion" ran to meet them with loud barks of welcome.

"Why, here are the wanderers!" declared the soldier, laughingly, but for a moment Grandma Vincent could hardly believe that the barefooted, bedraggled little girl who called, " Oh, Grandma, we've been lost," was the neat little Annette who had run down the path a few hours ago.

Kathy was almost too tired to speak, and Grandma and Marrilla nearly carried the little girls up the steps, while the soldier said that he would tell Kathy's parents that their little daughter was safe with Madame Vincent. "Mr. Down will drive over early in the morning, I'm sure," he called back, as he rode off toward New York. But Madame Vincent hardly realized that he had gone, for she was helping the girls up the wide staircase.

Annette and Kathy were too tired to tell their story that night. Marrilla and Grandma helped them undress, and before Marrilla could bring the bowls of bread and milk that Grandma had suggested, they were both fast asleep, and very soon the big house was quiet, the lights extinguished and its mistress alone was awake, wondering what explanation Annette would make of the day's adventures. For Madame Vincent now felt sure that the girls had opened the gate and let the colt out and had then endeavored to make him return.

Kathy woke up very early the next morning and dressed quietly without awakening Annette. As she stood near the chamber-window she could look out along the road leading to New York, and she saw a chaise rapidly approaching.

"It's my father," she thought, and tiptoed from the room, ran down the stairs and was on the front porch before the chaise had turned into the driveway.

Mr. Down's face was very grave as he greeted his little daughter. On the previous day he had secured a seaworthy schooner for the voyage to Bermuda, and Kathy's absence from home would cause a delay in all his plans for a prompt removal of his goods and his family from New York.

"Oh, Father, I forgot that Mother did not want me to come here, truly I did," pleaded Kathy as her father stepped from the chaise and stood beside her, and before Mr. Down could respond the little girl was telling the story of letting the brown colt out "for a walk in the garden," and of all that had followed.

Madame Vincent, at the noise of wheels on the driveway, had come to the door, and as she heard Kathy's story her face brightened. She realized that neither of the little girls had intended to be mischievous, and as Kathy finished telling her father of the long, tiresome chase after "Sir Guy," the little girl heard a friendly voice behind her say:

"Poor children! I am sure, Kathy, that your father will think I was a very careless person not to take better care of you," and Madame Vincent bowed smilingly to "Tory Down," thinking to herself that with her brown colt named for a British General and a Loyalist on her front steps it was indeed proof that peace was nearly established between England and America.

Mr. Down made his best bow to this friendly white-haired lady who seemed so fond of his little daughter and agreed to let Kathy remain until the following day, and drove away wishing to himself that he need not take his family to a far-off island, and perhaps regretting that he had made his friends among the enemies of America.

Kathy was now her own happy self again, and as she sat at breakfast beside Grandma Vincent, for Grandma had decided to let Annette sleep, she told her of their adventures of the previous day, and added thoughtfully:

"Something always happens when Annette and I plan to have a whole happy day."

"Well, to-day is Sunday, and if you and Annette are willing, I think I can plan a happy day for you and nothing happen to spoil it," Grandma responded smilingly.

"Yes, indeed," Kathy agreed. "Will you tell us just as soon as Annette comes down-stairs?"

"I am down-stairs now," they heard someone say, and they looked up to see a very sober little girl standing in the doorway.

"Oh, Annette, I have told your grandma all about it. And my father says I may stay until to-morrow night!" exclaimed Kathy, springing up from her seat at the table and running to meet her friend.

Annette looked anxiously toward her grandmother, for the little girl felt that she had been to blame in setting the colt free. But Grandma was smiling as if she had no thought of blame, and Annette gave a long sigh of relief as she took her place at the table and looked approvingly at the steaming bowl of porridge that Marrilla hastened to set before her.

After breakfast Grandma suggested that Kathy should put on one of Annette's muslin dresses, as Kathy's was soiled and torn from yesterday's adventure. "Then come out on the veranda for the morning's service," said Madame Vincent, and in a short time both the little girls were beside her in their dainty summer gowns, their brown curls tied back with white ribbons and looking as happy as if they had forgotten all about the hardships that they had passed through; and when Grandma Vincent declared that they looked enough alike to be sisters, Annette and Kathy were quite sure that their happy day had really begun.

"Sit here by me," said Grandma, as she placed herself on the cushioned bench at the end of the veranda, and the girls quickly obeyed. Their thoughts were full of the long day before them, and they were eager to know what Grandma Vincent had planned for their pleasure, but as they sat down they noticed that she held two small books, and that Marrilla stood in the open doorway, while Grimm was coming up the path.

"You see, my dears, I cannot always go to church on Sunday mornings, so I have a little service by myself. Grimm and Marrilla like to have me read to them, and perhaps you will like to sing this with me," said Madame Vincent, and she handed one of the small books to Annette, and the little group sang:

> "*Where'er Thy people meet,*
> *Appears Thy mercy-seat;*
> *Where'er they seek Thee, Thou art found,*
> *And every place is hallowed ground.*"

After this Madame Vincent read the story of Daniel in the lion's den, to which the girls listened eagerly. It seemed to them a wonderful and beautiful thing that the wild beasts could understand Daniel's innocence, and that he was safe with them.

The little white dog had established himself at his mistress's feet and, with his head tilted a little to one side, appeared to be listening to every word.

When the reading was over Grimm and Marrilla disappeared, and Grandma Vincent told the girls stories of her Dutch grandparents, who had built that very house. "And my grandmother's name was 'Annette,'" she reminded her little granddaughter, "and this and all the farms were then called 'boweries.'"

Then she told them that only the previous week three Indian squaws, accompanied by two little Indian girls, had come to the farm to gather the sweet grass that grew in the fields. This was interesting news to Annette and Kathy, and they wished they might have seen these visitors. The girls were both tired from their long chase of the day before, and they found it very pleasant to lean back on the cushioned bench and listen to the stories of far-off times.

Kathy felt pleased and grateful that Annette never seemed to remember that she was the daughter of a Tory. As they sat together that pleasant June morning Kathy recalled the many times Annette had defended her against the taunts and unkindness of other children. "And she always shares her good times with me," thought Kathy, and turned to smile radiantly at her friend, resolving never to forget her loyalty and kindness.

It was dinner time before they knew it. And Marrilla had made tiny frosted cakes on purpose for the little visitors, and they had just left the dining-room when there was the sound of wheels on the driveway, and Madame Vincent said:

"Run and put on your hats, my dears. Grimm is ready to take you for a drive."

"But you are going too, Grandma!" exclaimed Annette.

"Yes, indeed. I will be ready in a moment," was the smiling response, and very soon the little party were driving along the pleasant country road.

Annette and Kathy sat side by side on the back seat, and Kathy told her friend that when she went to Bermuda she would write to her every day. "Then when ships return to New York I will send all the letters sealed up in a package," she said, and Annette promised that she, too, would write and send the letters to Kathy whenever she could.

"Cousin John could get some sailor who was going to Bermuda to take my letters, but I am afraid he wouldn't," she said, and at this Kathy's smile vanished, for she was sure that John disliked Annette's friendship for a Tory's daughter, and she rejoined soberly:

"If I don't ever receive a letter from you, Annette, I shall be sure you are my true friend just the same."

How quickly that afternoon passed! It had indeed been a happy day for the little girls, and when that evening Madame Vincent pointed out the constellations in the summer sky, showing them the "Wagon," "Gemini—the Twins," as well as the Belt of Orion and the Pleiades, Annette declared that it had been a beautiful day. "We will always remember it, won't we, Kathy?" she said, and Kathy nodded and responded:

"Yes, indeed, always."

CHAPTER XI

TWO LITTLE INDIAN GIRLS

THE day after Kathy's departure Annette awoke to the sound of rain on the leaves of the trees near her chamber windows, and Grandma Vincent came into the room with a dainty little jacket of pink wool, saying that Annette had better slip it over her thin summer dress before coming down-stairs, as the weather had suddenly grown cool.

When Annette entered the dining-room she exclaimed in surprised delight: "Oh, I am glad it is raining, it makes this room so pleasant," at which Madame Vincent laughed heartily.

"It is the fire, not the rain, dear child, that makes the room pleasant," she responded, for there was a blaze of fragrant apple-wood on the broad hearth that seemed to make the room bright and sunny.

There were two whole days of rain, but Grandma Vincent found so many things for Annette to do that the little girl did not mind the bad weather. The aprons for Lottie were finished, and Marrilla helped Annette make some creamed walnuts and candied strawberries to take home as a gift to her mother. "Lion," too, proved good company for the little girl, and Annette often thought that she would like the fat little dog for her very own.

Before the skies cleared Annette and Grandma Vincent had planned the entertainment for the July Fourth party of the coming week. Ever since Grandma Vincent had told Annette the story of Hendrik Hudson and his ship, the *Half Moon*, and of the friendly welcome the Indians had given the explorers, she had resolved to ask Grandma if they could not play a "make-believe" of Hudson's arrival as an amusement for the guests at the garden party on July Fourth, and when she made this suggestion Madame Vincent declared it to be a fine idea.

"You see, Grandma, Cousin John's boat can be the *Half Moon* and John can be Hendrik Hudson. He can have little Peter Davidson and Betty Mason's two brothers for his crew, and Delia and Betty and I can be Indian squaws and cook a dinner for the white men," suggested Annette eagerly, and Madame Vincent said she thought that the idea was excellent.

"You can talk it over with your mother when you get home," she said.

The remainder of Annette's visit passed very quickly, and when early on Saturday morning her father came to take her home she declared the week to have been a very short time.

"But you will come to Cherry Street for our Fourth of July party, will you not, Grandma? And that will soon be here," she said, as she took her seat in the chaise beside her father.

Grandma promised, and then called to "Lion," who was trying to climb into the chaise beside Annette.

"Oh, Grandma, may not 'Lion' come with us for a visit?" asked Annette.

"Indeed he may if you want to bother with him, my dear," responded Madame Vincent, so the little dog was lifted to the seat beside Annette and settled down, evidently well pleased to be leaving the only home he had ever known.

"Perhaps Grandma means to give 'Lion' to me for my very own," said Annette as they started off toward home.

As they rode along Mr. Vincent told his little daughter of the various names by which New York had been known. "It was Manhattan in early days, and then the Dutch called it New Netherlands," he said, and Annette asked him what name the Indians had called the Hudson River.

"Co-ha-te-yah," responded her father.

Annette wished she dared ask her father if Merchant Down had sailed away to Bermuda, but she knew that such a question would betray Kathy's secret, so she did not mention her friend until she told her mother the story of their adventure with the brown colt, and of the happy Sunday with Grandma Vincent.

"Mr. Down's servant left a package here yesterday for you; it is in the lower drawer of the highboy," said Mrs. Vincent, and Annette ran eagerly to the tall chest of drawers, drew out the lower one and there lay a small package neatly wrapped in white paper. But as Annette picked it up her smile vanished.

"Oh, I cannot open it until September first. See, Mother, dear, Kathy has written 'For Annette. Not to be opened until September first.'"

"Well, Kathy has surely sent your birthday present in good season. September is two months ahead," responded Mrs. Vincent smilingly, but she wondered a little why Kathy had not kept the gift until Annette's birthday arrived.

"I do wonder what it is," said Annette, as she returned the package to the lower drawer. Her face had grown very serious, for she now realized that the time for Kathy's departure must be near at hand or she would not have sent the birthday gift.

"Lion" kept very close to Annette. There was a large Maltese cat in the kitchen, who made life in the Cherry Street house a dangerous adventure for the small white dog, and "Lion" was already regretting his departure from the safety of home, and felt Annette to be his only friend.

"We must make our plans for July Fourth at once," said Mrs. Vincent. "What did Grandma suggest?"

"I thought of something myself, Mother," said Annette, her face brightening at the remembrance of Hendrik Hudson, and Mrs. Vincent smiled her approval as she listened to her little daughter's plan, and agreed that it would be sure to entertain their guests.

"But it will all depend on your Cousin John's help," she reminded Annette, "and he will need some time to prepare his boat. Perhaps he may come in this afternoon and then we will ask him."

That afternoon Annette and her mother made a list of the guests to be invited to the garden party.

"On Monday morning you and Lottie can call and ask our friends," said Mrs. Vincent, and then added: "I am sorry, dear, that you cannot ask your friend Kathy. But you see we are asking the families of our friends loyal to America's rights, and we cannot ask a Tory to help us celebrate our Independence Day."

Annette understood this. She did not feel disappointed, for she now felt very sure that Kathy would soon leave New York, perhaps even before the day of the party.

John appeared late that afternoon and listened to his little cousin's story of Hendrik Hudson and the *Half Moon*, and when she had finished he good-naturedly promised to do his best to make the *Fleetwing* resemble the *Half Moon*, and to look as much like the bold explorer Hudson as possible.

"I'd like better to have the New York Tea Party over again," he declared. "There is great talk of Boston's Tea Party, but we had one of our own, right in this harbor, on April 21st, 1774, don't forget that, Annette; when the Sons of Liberty boarded the English ship *Vancy* and made her weigh anchor and take her cargo of tea back to England."

But Annette was more interested just then in her cousin's promise to represent Hendrik Hudson than in his story of the early days of the Revolution. It sometimes seemed to the little girl that all John thought about was the welfare and honor of America, and she often wondered if she would ever have an opportunity to prove her own loyalty.

"Perhaps you will do something fine for America, something that will always be remembered, John," she said soberly, as her tall cousin said "Good-bye."

"Perhaps so, and you must be ready to help," he rejoined laughingly, as he ran down the garden path to the landing where his boat was moored. Annette looked after him, thinking that if such a time ever came she would be ready.

Early on Monday morning Lottie and Annette started out to invite the guests for July Fourth. Mrs. Vincent had decided to ask only their nearest friends, but there were about ten houses to visit, and it was noon before Annette had finished. She would rap at the door and ask if she might see "the mistress of the house, if you please," and then when the lady appeared Annette would curtsey and say: "Good-morning. My mother sends her compliments, and she will be most happy if you and your family will come to our house at two o'clock on the afternoon of July Fourth and spend the afternoon."

The invitations were all smilingly accepted, and at Betty Mason's and Delia Davidson's, Annette saw her girl friends and told them of her plan, and they enthusiastically promised their help and that of their brothers.

Delia walked nearly home with Annette talking over the celebration of America's independence, and just as she reached St. George Square and had said good-bye, and as she turned to go home, she called back: "I'm glad you are not going to ask those Tories, the Downs."

Annette could feel her face flush angrily. It was not that she was a disloyal child, for she knew of the great sacrifices the American people had made for justice, but that Delia should rejoice that Kathy was not to be included in a good time with the other girls made Annette wish that she could call back, "Kathy *is* coming," but she could not do this, so she made no response, and hurried on toward home, wishing with all her heart that there was some way in which she could make up to her little Tory friend for the unfair treatment of her playmates.

The next two days were very busy days in the Vincent household. Mrs. Vincent and Lottie were baking cakes and custards, while during his spare time Mr. Vincent worked in the garden building a number of "wigwams" of poles and brush, which were to form the Indian village. Annette helped her father with this work, and Delia and Betty came to ask about their part in the "play," as they now called Annette's entertainment.

John and the boys who were to form his crew were very secret about their plans. And John would only laugh and shake his head when Annette questioned him.

"Wait until the Fourth," was all he would say.

The morning of the Fourth was fair and sunny, and as Annette looked from her open window and saw the circle of wigwams at the foot of the garden she laughed happily.

"It is going to be the very best time of all the summer," she told herself, " even better than the picnic at Staten Island, or the visit at Grandma's." But this made her think of Kathy, of whom she had not heard since they said good-bye at Greenwich Village.

Grandma Vincent arrived in time for the noon-day meal, greatly to "Lion's" delight. He no longer followed Annette, but kept close to his mistress as if determined not to be again separated from her.

Early in the afternoon before the arrival of the guests Annette ran down for a look at the "Indian village," and as she neared the wigwam nearest the landing she heard someone call: "Annette, Annette," and in a moment saw Kathy Down peering cautiously out from the opening.

"Oh, Kathy!" she exclaimed.

"Sshh!" cautioned Kathy. "No one must see me. I've come to say 'good-bye,' dear Annette. All our goods are loaded on a schooner in the lower bay, and to-night we are to go on board. But I couldn't bear not to see you once more."

Annette was now inside the wigwam, and the two little friends were silent for a moment at the thought that the time had really come when Kathy was to start on the voyage to Bermuda.

"But, Kathy, you must stay to my party," she declared. "Promise you will. You can start for home in good season. Listen, Kathy! You know everyone says that we look alike. Well, I am to dress as an Indian girl, in a little skirt made of deerskin, and moccasins, and a head-dress of turkey feathers. And Mother made two costumes just alike, and then Betty had fixed one for herself. So, Kathy, you can wear the one my mother planned for Betty, and we will stain our faces with the stuff John has fixed and pull our hair well over our faces. Then I can be careful and hide when you walk about, and you can hide when I am in sight. Oh, Kathy! It will be fun. No one will find out about it. Promise you will. I'll bring the Indian dress down for you and you can put it on in this wigwam."

As Annette talked Kathy's face brightened. The thought of one more happy afternoon with her best friend made her forget the dangers of such a plan, and she promptly agreed.

"But I must start for home in good season," she warned Annette, who hardly noticed what Kathy was saying, for she was in a hurry to return to the house and secure Kathy's costume before the arrival of Betty and Delia and the other girls and boys who were to take part in the play.

"Keep way back in the wigwam, Kathy," she cautioned, and then ran toward the house.

Everyone was too busy to pay attention to Annette, and in a short time she was back at the wigwam and she and Kathy stained each other's faces with the brown coloring that John had prepared. A head-dress of turkey feathers nodded on each little head, and when they drew their brown hair well over their faces, as Annette had suggested, and stood side by side no one could have told which was Annette and which was Kathy.

"It's going to be fun. Remember just to nod and grunt if anyone speaks to you," cautioned Annette, and the two girls chuckled happily at the thought of the joke they were about to play on all the guests of the afternoon.

"Hide, Kathy! Quick, here come Delia and Betty," whispered Annette, running out from the wigwam to meet the girls, who came hurrying down the path.

CHAPTER XII

By half-past two o'clock the guests were all assembled near the "Indian village." The boys were all dressed as Indian braves, Annette, Delia and Betty were dressed as squaws, but the other little girl visitors wore their pretty summer muslins and one exclaimed laughingly: "Annette is everywhere! I saw her at the landing, and then as I looked around she was close beside me."

"Yes," responded Delia, to whom the little girl was speaking, "I don't know how she gets about so quickly," for Annette and Kathy were carrying out their plan very successfully, and as yet were unsuspected.

It was the middle of the afternoon when there was a little murmur of applause as a two-masted, high-sterned vessel appeared in the river nearly opposite the landing. In the bow of the vessel stood John dressed in a high-crowned hat, a long belted coat and high boots. He held up one hand to screen his eyes as he looked toward the shore, as if beholding a strange land for the first time.

Just behind him stood little Peter Mason and the two Davidson boys dressed in the same fashion and

125

endeavoring to look like bold explorers from far-off Holland.

John had worked hard to make his boat and crew resemble the pictures he had seen of the *Half Moon*. He had built up a high stern on the *Fleetwing* and added a temporary extra mast, and he was well pleased by the praise and approval of the older guests and the delight and surprise of the boys and girls, who realized more clearly than ever before that Manhattan's shores had once been a wild region inhabited only by Indians.

Hendrik Hudson was warmly welcomed, and he and his men came on shore to feast with the Indian braves and the white settlers. Betty Mason, Delia and Annette brought the cool strawberry-flavored drinks, the sandwiches and frosted cakes, the custards and whipped cream-puffs that Mrs. Vincent had made ready for her guests, and more than one noticed that Annette really seemed to be in two places at once.

"Who is the other girl dressed just like you, Annette?" John asked laughingly, as an Indian squaw brought him a well-filled plate of cream-puffs. But the girl he supposed to be Annette, who was really Kathy, vanished so quickly that John looked after her in surprise.

Kathy and Annette would now and then meet for a moment out of sight of the others and whisper their delight at the success of Annette's plan, for until John's question had alarmed Kathy they had been sure that no one suspected them.

The afternoon went by happily. If the Indian squaws found their costumes too warm for a July day they made no complaint. The older members of the company told stories of the days when New York was a Dutch colony of log houses, and a stone fort as a protection against the Indians, while John was the centre of a group composed of "Indian braves" and the crew of the *Half Moon*, to whom he was telling of the Battle of Golden Hill; Golden Hill being a little rise of ground on John Street near the centre of the city, where, on January 18th, 1770, was struck the first blow of the American Revolution, when English soldiers endeavored to destroy a Liberty Pole erected by New York citizens and were driven away by loyal men.

The younger boys listened eagerly to John's account of the courage of the Sons of Liberty. They all considered John to be a hero, as they knew he had sailed to far-off ports, and they felt proud to be his companions in this celebration of July Fourth, America's Independence Day.

Twilight was approaching when Lottie came hurrying down the path saying that Mr. Down's servant was at the door and would like to speak to Miss Annette.

It was Kathy to whom she gave the message, and the frightened little girl dared not face Phyllis, whom she was sure would instantly recognize her, but she ran up toward the house and hid beneath a lilac bush, while the surprised Lottie, on turning for a look at the *Half Moon*, found herself facing Annette.

"Ma grashus sakes, Missie, ain' I jes' tells yo' to step to de fron' do'r an' spik to dat wuthless nigger o' Massa Down?" she exclaimed.

For a moment Annette looked at Lottie in surprise. "What does she want?" she whispered.

"She's a-huntin' af'er dat Miss Kathy. I tells her plain dat dis ain' no Tory pahty," replied Lottie proudly, "an' dat I ain' seen no Miss Kathy. But she's turrible 'cited, an' say she *mus'* see you, so I reckon you'd better step along."

Annette hardly knew what to do. She remembered that Kathy's wide flower-trimmed hat lay hidden in the wigwam, and in a moment she resolved to endeavor to save Kathy from any trouble caused by her own plan for deceiving the others. She would put on Kathy's hat and try and make Phyllis believe that she was Kathy, and thus give Kathy time to take off her disguise and return to Nassau Street.

"I'll be there in a moment," she told Lottie and ran into the wigwam. An instant later she darted past Lottie, ran through the hall to the front door, where Phyllis stood on the shadowy porch.

The wide hat concealed Annette's face from the anxious servant, and she seized the little girl's hand and drew her rapidly down the steps.

"My lan', Missie Kathy, wot you a-t'inkin' 'bout to run off de berry day yo' fo'ks is ready to sail? An' all rigged up like yo' be! Yo' ma's 'bout crazy. She's on de ship dis minnit, an' yo' pa is a-waitin' in a boat down ter de shore fer me ter fetch yo'. I tells him I knowed jes' whar to fin' yo'. My lan'!" And without waiting for any response, Phyllis talked on of all the hard work she had accomplished that afternoon.

"An' now de house am closed, an' by mawin' we'll be on our way to whar dar ain' no 'Merican fo'ks to make trubble fer us," she said, turning into a narrow street that led toward the shore.

Annette began to wonder what would happen to Kathy. She felt sure that her little friend had heard Lottie's message, and that Kathy would instantly start for Nassau Street, but if the house was closed and Mrs. Down on board ship, what would become of the little girl?

"Oh, Phyllis, aren't we going to Nassau Street?" she asked in a hoarse whisper.

"Dar, you've cotched cold! Mah sakes! I cyn't hahdly hear yo'. No, Missie, yo' pa tells me to fetch yo' right down to de place whar he's waitin' wid de boat ter take us to de ship. I reckon yo's gwine ter get scolded, Missie," concluded the negress.

Clouds were gathering in the twilight sky, and it had suddenly grown too dark to clearly distinguish any object not close at hand, and Phyllis hurried on anxious to reach the shore; and before Annette could decide what it was best to do a tall figure appeared directly in front of them, and she heard Phyllis exclaim:

"H'ar Miss Kathy, Massa Down," and Annette's hand was grasped finely by Kathy's father.

"There's no time to lose," he declared. "I'm afraid there's a storm coming up before we can get on board ship. You have made us great trouble, Kathy," he added, as they reached the water's edge where a boat with two sailors on board was waiting.

Annette now realized there was no time to lose. She must tell Mr. Down that Kathy was probably at that very moment on her way to Nassau Street.

"Oh! Please—" she began, but Mr. Down instantly silenced her.

"Keep quiet, Katherine. You can tell your story to your mother."

"But I must tell you—" Annette exclaimed, as Mr. Down lifted her on board the boat, where she was quickly followed by Phyllis, and a moment later they were clear from the shore, and the sailors bent to their oars and sent the boat rapidly through the water.

Mr. Down was in the bow, while Annette and Phyllis were seated in the stern.

"I don't want to go. I mustn't! I'm not Kathy Down, I am—" Annette declared, pulling away from Phyllis, and endeavoring to stand on her feet only to be pulled back and scolded by the puzzled negress who wondered what "possessed" her young mistress, and hardly knew what to do. The rain had begun to fall before the boat reached Mr. Down's vessel. One of the sailors lifted Annette on board, and Phyllis climbed up after her, and at that moment Mr. Down exclaimed:

"Here comes a boat after us," and a voice called:

"Boat ahoy! A passenger for Mr. Down."

"Oh! It's John! It's John!" cried Annette, dancing about on the slippery deck; and a small boat darted up beside the ship to the surprise and bewilderment of Mr. Down, for here was another little girl calling: "Father! Father!" and a queer figure in a high crowned hat that made Mr. Down wonder who it could be, as John hurriedly explained that Phyllis had taken the wrong girl, and that Kathy had asked him to follow them.

The rain ceased as suddenly as it had begun, the sky cleared, and the summer stars shone down on the queer company gathered on the deck of the little schooner. The two " Indian girls," John in his Dutch costume, while Phyllis in her blue dress and white turban, frightened and puzzled, looked from one to the other of the little girls, hardly knowing which one to claim for her little mistress.

There was a hurried explanation in which Annette falteringly told of her plan for one more good time with Kathy. "And I came with Phyllis to give Kathy a chance to get back to Nassau Street. I did not mean to make so much trouble," she concluded.

"Say good-bye to your friend, Kathy," said Mr. Down sharply. "We have no more time to lose."

For a moment Kathy and Annette clung together, but they said no word of good-bye; then John drew his little cousin toward the side of the vessel, helped her into the small boat, picked up his oars and with a strong pull sent his little craft clear of the ship.

"Good-bye, Annette. Dear Annette, good-bye," called Kathy, and looking back Annette could see a shadowy little figure near the ship's rail, and called back: "Good-bye, dear Kathy."

John did not speak to his cousin until they landed. Then he told her that Phyllis had hardly left the Cherry Street house before Kathy had come running to him and told all the story, and begged him to go with her after Annette and Phyllis.

"We were close behind you when Mr. Down's boat left the shore," said John, "and I hailed him then, but could not make him hear. I had to search for a boat, too, and began to think it was no use to try to rescue you."

Annette hardly heard what John was saying. She was thinking of Kathy, now sailing away not again to return to New York.

But John thought it important that Annette should realize how much trouble she had made by her friendship for a Tory girl, and continued:

"If your guests knew that a Tory girl was one of the company this afternoon they would think little of your patriotism, Annette. Suppose you had really been carried off on that Tory vessel, what would have become of you?"

Annette was very tired and unhappy, but she knew herself to be a loyal American girl, as well as a true friend to Kathy, and she answered sharply:

"Wait and see if I am not as patriotic as you are, Cousin John."

"Yes, with the war over, and Governor George Clinton doing his best to get English troops out of the country, it's an easy matter now to be a patriot," sneered the boy scornfully.

"Perhaps I can prove it some way," Annette insisted. "You wait and see," and John said no more, for they were now at the door of the Cherry Street house, and after seeing Annette safely at home John vanished, leaving his cousin to tell her mother and father the story of the evening.

CHAPTER XIII

VISITORS

THE week following the garden party was not a very happy time for Annette. Every day she thought of Kathy, and often opened the drawer that held her friend's birthday gift and looked at the neat little package, wondering what message it might contain from her far-off friend, and wishing that September was not so distant a time that she might open the package.

And besides missing Kathy, Annette's thoughts were troubled by the remembrance of her Cousin John's assertion that Annette was not loyal to America. With all her heart Annette hoped that the time might come when she could prove her patriotism to her cousin; and such a time did come, although not as soon as the little girl hoped for.

"Lion" had been as eager to return to Greenwich Village with his mistress as he had been rejoiced to accompany Annette to Cherry Street. It was evident the little, fat white dog had learned that home was the best place, but Annette missed him and began to wish that she had a dog of her own. "Matilda," as the big Maltese cat was named, objected to being a pet, and

134

kept very close to Lottie, or ran off into the garden whenever Annette endeavored to make friends with her, so that at last the little girl decided that a dog was a much more satisfactory friend; but, as "Lion" was in Greenwich Village, Annette amused herself with her two dolls, "Stella" and "Vesta," taking them into the garden on warm afternoons, and making new gowns and hats for each of them of strips of silk and lace from her mother's "piece-bag."

It was a week after the garden party when Delia Davidson and Betty Mason, both wearing their best summer dresses, came up the steps of the Cherry Street house and when Lottie opened the door primly inquired if " Miss Annette" was at home.

Lottie ushered them into the parlor, and hurried into the garden to find her little mistress.

"Dar's two fine young ladies a-callin' on you, Miss Annette," she announced solemnly, and then returned to her kitchen chuckling with satisfaction over "de grown-up way dose gals act," while Annette, with both her dolls in her arms, came running into the house. But before entering the parlor Annette seated "Stella" and "Vesta" on the broad settle in the hall, smoothed her hair, and then walked sedately into the cool pleasant front room.

Delia and Betty had seated themselves on a sofa opposite the door, and as Annette entered they both stood up, curtseyed, and said, in what they intended to be a very dignified manner, "Good-afternoon, Miss Vincent. We have come to make our party call."

Nothing could have pleased Annette more, as she delighted in "make-believes," and, for the first time since Kathy Down's departure, she felt a thrill of delight in the companionship of playmates, and she, in her turn, curtseyed, and advanced with out-stretched hand, saying:

"I am indeed pleased to see you, Miss Davidson and Miss Mason. Will you not be seated?"

But a giggle from Delia made all three of the little girls forget their attempt to act like "grown-ups," and in a moment they were all talking eagerly, although Betty did not forget to take her knitting from her fine silk work-bag and to knit while she chattered about "Hendrik Hudson," and the good time they had enjoyed at Annette's garden party.

Both Delia and Betty spoke of Annette's quickness in being "in two places at once," on July Fourth.

"Truly, you were," declared Betty soberly. "For you brought me a custard, and almost at the same minute I saw you in the door of one of the wigwams. I don't see how you managed it."

But Annette kept her seat. She had resolved that no one outside her own family should know of Kathy's part in the celebration of America's Independence Day; and as Delia and Betty were both eager to tell Annette of the departure of the Downs and of a party

Sir Guy Carleton had given for them on the afternoon before the Downs sailed, they did not notice Annette's failure to respond to Betty's question.

"And Sir Guy invited Kathy," continued Delia, "because it seems he had a fine gift for her, a locket and chain. But Kathy could not be found, so Sir Guy's servant told our Nick, although the Downs searched everywhere for her."

"And did not Kathy get her locket?" Annette questioned anxiously.

"Oh, I suppose so. Probably her mother took it for her," responded Delia.

"But the strange part of it all is that no one saw Kathy all that afternoon," said Betty, looking at Annette so sharply that Annette could feel her face flush.

"Well, nobody saw the Downs move all their things. 'Twas all done secretly," said Delia, "but we did not mean to talk about the Downs," she added quickly. "I am going to have a birthday party, Annette, on the last day of July, and I hope you will come. I am only asking my best friends," she added, "and you must not give me any present because this is to be a new kind of a birthday party, and presents would spoil it."

Annette promised all that Delia suggested in regard to the party. Guests were to arrive at three o'clock in the afternoon, and to remain for an early supper.

"Of course I cannot tell you what the surprise will be," said Delia, evidently well pleased with her secret; and Betty and Annette hastened to respond that of course Delia could not tell them anything so important.

Just as Annette's visitors were thinking that they must start for home Mrs. Vincent came into the room, closely followed by Lottie bringing a tray with glasses of raspberry-shrub and a plate of sugar cookies.

"Just as if we're really grown-up visitors," thought Delia, as she spread a tiny fringed napkin over her blue muslin, and helped herself to a cooky.

The young visitors soon took their departure in as formal a manner as they had arrived, and Mrs. Vincent declared them to be well-mannered girls, adding: "I hope you will be good friends with Delia and Betty, Annette."

"Oh, yes, Mother," rejoined the little girl, "only they are so nearly grown up. Why, they are both thirteen years old, and I am not eleven until September. Kathy was just my age," she concluded, a little mournfully. But Mrs. Vincent made no response; she hoped that Annette would soon be reconciled to the absence of her little Tory friend; and after the visit of Delia and Betty, Annette was more cheerful. She looked forward to Delia's birthday party, wondering what the surprise could be, and began to realize that, after all, September first, when she could open Kathy's package, was not so very far away.

During the warm July days Mrs. Vincent and Annette spent many hours in the pleasant garden. In the early morning hours before the heat of the day began they worked among the neat rows of vegetables, pulling up weeds, or gathering peas and beans, young beets or fresh lettuce for the midday meal. Then later on Annette had her study hour on the shady porch. During the years when the British Army occupied New York the schools for American children were neglected, and many children were taught at home; so Mrs. Vincent helped her little daughter with lessons in arithmetic, grammar and geography; and at the beginning of 1783 Annette had been eager to study the French language, greatly to her father's satisfaction; and as Mr. Vincent could read and speak the French language he was always ready to help his little daughter over the puzzling verbs, and the pronunciation.

Beside the lessons Annette was expected to perform certain household duties: to set the table for tea, to dust her own room and keep it in order, to mend her stockings, and often there were household errands for her to do; so with these many pleasant occupations, her dolls to play with and occasional sails in the *Fleetwing*, the July days passed quickly and Delia's birthday, with its "surprise" for her guests, arrived and found Annette nearly consoled for Kathy's absence.

Americans were becoming more and more anxious for the departure of the British soldiers from New York. The families of Tories were leaving the city as rapidly as possible, but Sir Guy Carleton's troops continued in their camps on the Bowery, while their officers occupied the finest mansions in the city. Annette had not seen Sir Guy Carleton since meeting him on the morning of her drive to Greenwich Village, and when she recalled her visit to the house of the British General and his friendly reception she wondered why so kindly a man could be an enemy to America's rights. She often wondered if she would ever speak with him again, and if he remembered that he had asked a little American girl to be his friend.

The day of Delia's birthday was a perfect summer's day. There was a cool little breeze coming from the harbor, and Annette could hardly wait for the hour to come for her to start for Broad Street, where Delia's father lived.

Lottie was to see that Annette reached the Davidson house safely, and call for her little mistress at twilight; and at two o'clock Annette stood on the front steps of the Cherry Street house all ready to start. She wore her best white muslin dress, and her white hat with its wreath of pink rosebuds, her silk mitts, and open-work stockings, and she carried the pretty parasol.

Lottie looked at her little mistress approvingly as they walked along the well-shaded streets. The faithful negress was sure that no other little girl at the party would compare with Annette.

They had turned into Wall Street when a clatter of horses' hoofs, and the jingle of bridle-reins made Annette look up quickly, and there, almost beside her, rode Sir Guy and a number of English officers in their fine uniforms.

There was a smile on the British General's face as Annette curtseyed. It was not often that any American child greeted him, and he drew rein and said:

"Good-day. I am sure this is my little friend Annette Vincent."

"Yes, Sir Guy. And I am on my way to a party," responded Annette.

"And you have not forgotten your promise, I trust?" said the General, holding his spirited horse with a firm hand.

"No, indeed. But, if you please, Sir Guy, are you not going to take your soldiers back to England very soon?" ventured the little girl, remembering that her father had said there could be no prosperity or freedom in New York until it was clear of British soldiers.

For a moment Sir Guy's smile disappeared, but he looked down kindly at the little girl as he responded:

"As soon as may be we'll set sail for England."

There was a little murmur of laughter among his officers as Annette declared with evident delight:

"That will be splendid!" and Sir Guy smiled again, as he said: "But we will meet again before I go, Miss America," and with a word to his horse he rode off down the street toward the Battery where the English flag still waved from the tall flagpole.

"My lan', Missie! How yo' dar' ter 'vise dat General," gasped Lottie, looking with startled eyes at Annette.

But the little girl made no response. She was thinking that if her Cousin John had heard her ask Sir Guy Carleton to leave New York that he would know that she was loyal to America. "But of course John thinks that to be patriotic means more than to ask a question," thought Annette, with so sober a face that Lottie was glad they were at the steps of the Davidson house where she could take leave of her little mistress and return to Cherry Street.

Delia was at the door and welcomed Annette, saying:

"Lay your hat and parasol on the hall table, Annette; Betty is waiting for you on the back porch," and Delia turned to smile her greeting to the Van Steldt girls, twin sisters, of Delia's own age. They were always dressed exactly alike, and thought it a fine game to be mistaken for each other.

Annette ran out to the back porch where she found Betty seated on the top step, knitting in hand. It was evidently one of Betty's days when she intended to be as "grown-up" as possible, for while the other girls were already playing a game of "Hunt the Slipper" in the garden, Betty looked down at them now and then as if amused by their childish play, and kept steadily on with her knitting. As Annette looked at the flying needles she did not wonder that Betty had knit the stockings worn by the Mason family for the past year. "I believe Betty could knit in her sleep," Annette thought admiringly.

But at the sight of Annette Betty jumped up, put her knitting away, and exclaimed:

"I am so glad you have come, Annette. Delia wants you and me to help her with her 'surprise.' Did she tell you what it was to be?"

"No, Delia has not said a word about it. What is it, Betty?" Annette responded, looking expectantly at Betty.

CHAPTER XIV

"THE OTHER SIX"

"You will know in a moment," Betty replied, "when the other six girls arrive."

"'The other six'?" repeated Annette questioningly.

"Why, yes. You see, Delia has invited the Van Steldt twins, and Isabel Clifton and you and me, and with Delia that makes six," responded Betty.

"Oh, Betty! Of course it does," Annette rejoined impatiently, "but what has it to do with the 'surprise,' and who are the 'other six'?"

"Well," said Betty, rolling up her knitting and putting it carefully into the bag, "I guess you will know in a minute for I'm sure I hear the 'other six,'" and before Annette could ask another question she heard a murmur of voices in the hall and Delia appeared in the doorway leading a little girl whom Annette was sure that she had never seen before.

"Betty and Annette, here is my little friend Milly," said Delia, smiling down at the thin-faced, solemn-eyed child whom she held by the hand and who bobbed her head in response to the introduction. Directly behind Delia stood five other little girls, none of them over ten years of age, and all of them dressed in ugly gowns of coarse grey cloth. They were all barefooted, and all had their hair cut short. Annette knew at once that these little girls had come from the asylum that cared for homeless children, and quickly realized something of what Delia's "surprise" meant.

Delia called to Isabel Clifton and the twins, and they came running up from the garden and then Delia made a little "birthday speech," as she called it, saying that she had thought of a splendid way to make a birthday remembered.

"Here are six little girls who all say that they never had a birthday," said Delia, "so I have asked them here to become acquainted with you six older girls who do have birthdays. I am going to make a present of my own birthday to Milly," and she smiled at the solemn-eyed little girl who clasped Delia's hand a little more tightly, "and then each of you girls can choose one of the other five for your birthday girl," and Delia looked at the little group as if she were sure she had given them a most wonderful surprise, as indeed she had. "You choose first, Betty," she added, and Betty stepped forward and clasped the hand of a freckle-faced little girl with red hair.

"I choose Rachel," she announced promptly, and Rachel rewarded her with so grateful a smile that Betty was sure she had made a wise choice.

Annette chose a small dark-eyed girl whose name was Nancy, and in a few moments Delia's guests were all paired off, hand in hand.

"The other six," as Betty had called Delia's small visitors from the asylum, were at first rather shy and silent with their new friends, but as Delia and Milly led the way to the garden where Mrs. Davidson had spread a table with the birthday supper, their faces brightened and they began to ask eager questions.

"Do some girls have a birthday every year?" Nancy whispered to Annette, as they took their places at the round table.

"Yes, of course. Everybody does," replied Annette.

Nancy shook her head soberly. "Not in norphan 'sylums they don't. Nobody has 'em there," she said in a matter-of-fact tone.

"Well, Nancy, you shall have a birthday every year. You shall have mine."

For a moment Nancy smiled radiantly at so delightful a possibility, but her face grew serious again and she shook her head. "I wouldn't be so mean as to take yours," she said.

"I mean that we will both have the same day for our birthday," Annette hastened to explain. "You see, that is why Delia has asked us all here, to share birthdays. You and I will have ours together, on the first day of September! And Delia and Milly will have theirs to-day; and the other girls just the same.

When September first arrives you shall come and stay all day with me."

Nancy's face brightened as she listened to what seemed to her so beautiful a plan; and as Mrs. Davidson was now serving the creamed oysters, fresh rolls and saucers heaped with raspberries to each of the little guests, Nancy did not at once respond. It seemed a marvellous feast to the "other six," and when ices in the shape of peaches were brought, and a big frosted cake with fourteen candles, there were exclamations of surprise and delight. For although the asylum furnished shelter and food and clothing for as many homeless children as possible, it had found it difficult to provide for the children even the necessities during the British occupation of New York, and "the other six" had never before tasted such dainties as were now set before them, nor had they ever before seen such a thing as a birthday cake with lighted candles.

After each little guest had eaten a good-sized piece of the cake and finished her ice, Delia asked to be excused for a moment and ran into the house. In a few moments she was back again with a basket containing six neatly wrapped boxes. She gave one to Betty, to Annette, to each of the twins, and to Isabel Clifton, but as each of the girls received her box she saw written on it the name of the "birthday girl" she had chosen, and Annette quickly passed hers to

Nancy, and Delia gave a similar one to Milly, as the other girls handed theirs on to their companions.

"Not to be opened until you get home, remember," said Delia; and "the other six," holding the boxes very tightly, nodded and smiled as they promised.

"It's a doll for each one," Delia whispered to Annette.

After supper the girls played "Hide the Slipper" for a time, and then sat together in a circle while Delia told a wonderful story of a family of robins that lived in the tall elm tree. Milly and Nancy instantly recalled the robins they had seen in trees near the asylum, and resolved to watch them closely after this. Then Betty and Annette sang:

> *"Listen, a secret we will sing,*
> *Of fairies a-dozen, all in a ring.*
> *Each with a thistle-bloom and a gold crown—*
> *This may you see as the sun goes down."*

It was a gay little tune, and as Annette and Betty repeated the last two lines Delia and Isabel joined in, and in a moment the girls were all standing, and at a word from Delia they joined bands in a big ring and danced gaily around to the song.

"The other six" had never before heard of fairies, and Annette, Betty, as well as Delia, Isabel and the twins, were soon happily explaining to their companion what they believed about fairies.

At sunset Lottie appeared to take Annette home, and Mr. Davidson said he would drive the six little girls to the asylum.

It was a happy group that gathered on the Davidsons' porch to say their good-byes.

"The other six" had their precious boxes again, and as each one took her place in the carriage she was reminded of the date of the "birthday" that had been bestowed on her, and they called back happily that they would surely remember.

"I will see you soon, Nancy. I'll ask my mother if you may not come soon and make me a visit," Annette said, as she bade good-bye to her new friend.

"What is a 'visit'?" asked Nancy wonderingly; but there was not time to explain before the carriage started, so Annette called:

"I'll tell you when I come to see you."

As Annette bade Delia good-night, she said: "Your birthday has been beautiful, Delia, and the best 'surprise' anyone could have," and each of Delia's guests said the same, as they started for home with their thoughts filled with plans for the pleasure of the "birthday girl" whom Delia had given, as they all felt, into their special charge.

Annette was eager to reach home and tell her mother of Delia's wonderful birthday party, and to ask if Nancy might not come and stay with her for a long visit. As Annette recalled the happy faces of "the other six" she was sure that Delia's birthday party was the finest one possible to have; and she began to think that Delia Davidson was the finest girl she knew.

"Only she is so nearly grown up," reflected Annette regretfully, as she remembered the fourteen candles on Delia's birthday cake, and sent a longing thought to far-away Kathy whose birthday was so near her own.

As for the six little girls from the asylum they could hardly believe their own good fortune when they discovered that the mysterious packages each held a beautiful china doll dressed in white dotted muslin. Although the dresses were all alike each doll wore a sash of a different color. Nancy's doll had a blue sash, greatly to Nancy's delight, as Annette had worn a sash of that color. The young visitors told the story of Delia's birthday party to many of the younger and older girls who knew no other home than the asylum, and these others began to think that Nancy and her companions were very fortunate; but the account of their happy visit and the six dolls brought a new interest to all the children in the asylum, and when on the following day baskets of food arrived at the asylum from the families of Delia's friends there was a new cause for rejoicing. There was no doubt but that Delia had discovered a sure way to make her birthday remembered happily.

Mr. and Mrs. Vincent listened with great interest as Annette described the "surprise," and told them of "the other six" who did not know the meaning of a birthday party.

"And my girl is named Nancy, and she thinks she is eight years old. And her eyes are brown, and her hair is short; and oh, Mother, dear, may I ask her to come and visit me? I told her I would," said Annette eagerly.

"Why, yes, indeed. We will go to the asylum and see Nancy to-morrow," her mother agreed cheerfully. " I think Mrs. Davidson must be very proud of her daughter," she added, as Annette explained that Delia had made the plan when Mrs. Davidson had told her that she could choose her own birthday present.

"Yes, and Betty Mason said that when her birthday came she would ask 'the other six'; and Isabel Clifton is going to have them on her birthday, and so are the Van Steldt twins," responded Annette.

"And I suppose my little daughter will ask them on September first," said Mrs. Vincent, just as Annette had hoped that she would.

"Yes, Mother, dear. And may we go early to-morrow morning and bring Nancy home with us?"

Mrs. Vincent promised, and Annette went happily off to bed. It had been a wonderful day, she thought, as she recalled her meeting with Sir Guy Carleton, the good time at the birthday party, and last of all her mother's promise that Nancy should come for a visit.

"Nancy is the best part of it all," she decided. "It will be splendid to have a little girl stay right here in my own house with me."

CHAPTER XV

NANCY RUNS AWAY

"Mother, Nancy does not know what a 'visit' is," said Annette the next morning, as she and her mother entered the wide-seated chaise for their drive to the asylum.

"We must do our best then to have her discover that a real visit is one of the nicest things in the world," Mrs. Vincent responded.

"But all visits are 'real,'" said Annette, and her mother shook her head laughingly.

"No, my dear. The British soldiers who are in New York are visitors, but not 'real' visitors, because we do not want them and will rejoice to see them go. What I mean by a 'real' visit is to have someone come whom you are glad to welcome and for whom you wish to do everything in your power to make them happy."

"I see; and I can do lots of things for Nancy," declared Annette.

There was no trouble in regard to Nancy leaving the asylum for the visit of a week with the Vincents. The overworked matron declared that she wished all her charges could be asked for such a visit; and

Nancy, holding the precious doll, was lifted into the chaise beside her new friends.

"This is the beginning of your visit, Nancy," Annette explained, after she had introduced the silent little girl to her mother. "A 'visit' means that you go and stay with friends in their house, and have a lovely time; a real visit, I mean," she concluded.

Nancy did not speak. She sat very close to Annette, and now and then a little smile crept over her thin face. She wished that Milly, who slept beside her each night, might have come with her on this new and wonderful ride that was to end in a "visit," but not until the chaise stopped in front of the Cherry Street house and Mrs. Vincent said: "Hop out, children; and Annette, tell Lottie to give Nancy a glass of milk and some bread and honey," did the little asylum girl feel sure that such a beautiful thing as to stay with Annette was really true.

Nancy drank the milk thirstily, and Lottie again filled her glass; after she had eaten the bread and honey Annette led her up-stairs. A second bed had been put in Annette's chamber, where Nancy was to sleep, and on this bed lay a pretty white cotton dress with little pink rosebuds woven in it, and dainty undergarments and white stockings, while on the floor stood a pair of Annette's partly worn slippers that Lottie had blacked and polished until they looked like new.

"This is your bed, Nancy, and those are your clothes," said Annette eagerly, "and you are to put them right on."

"I'll wait for you on the back porch, Nancy," said Annette, and with a smiling nod to her little guest, she ran down-stairs.

It was not long before Nancy, still holding her doll as if fearing it was too valuable a possession to lose sight of for a moment, appeared on the porch; but it was a new Nancy. Dressed in the pretty gown and neat shoes, her short hair washed and brushed until it lay in little waves, her cheeks flushed and her eyes shining with happiness it was no wonder that Annette ran to meet her exclaiming:

"Why, Nancy! You are just as pretty as you can be," and kissed the little girl on each cheek.

It was the beginning of the happiest week Nancy had ever known. To have all the milk you wanted to drink, with fresh berries and hot rolls every morning, and a jar in the kitchen that, no matter how many cookies you took out, always had more spicy molasses snaps ready to be eaten, to play in the beautiful garden with Annette, and even to ride to Greenwich Village to see Grandma Vincent, all these things made the little asylum girl feel that the world was a much pleasanter place than she had thought; and when at the end of the week Annette told Nancy that she was to make a longer stay it would have been difficult to tell which of the two little girls seemed the happier.

"You are to stay until after our birthday," said Annette, "and your hair is not to be cut while you are here. Isn't that splendid!"

Nancy nodded, but remained silent. It seemed to Annette that she had never known a little girl who had so little to say.

"Why don't you talk more, Nancy? You don't talk half as much as I do," and Annette looked at her new friend a little anxiously.

"'Little girls should be seen and not heard,'" responded Nancy, gravely, repeating one of the asylum maxims she had so often heard.

"Oh, Nancy, that isn't what my mother thinks," and Nancy listened eagerly to Annette's assurance that there was no possible harm in talking, and before September arrived she had nearly forgotten all the asylum rules that had made life so difficult for a little girl. Nancy's hair now waved about her forehead and ears; she had gained in weight and was no longer the sober-faced little girl whom Annette had first seen at Delia's party. Mr. and Mrs. Vincent had grown very fond of their little visitor, and as Annette's birthday drew near they often talked over Nancy's future, for they both felt that it was hardly possible to let the little girl return to the asylum.

Annette and Nancy were told that they could do whatever they pleased to celebrate their birthday and Nancy had instantly exclaimed: "Could I ask Milly to spend the day?" and Mrs. Vincent had smilingly agreed.

"Why can we not have Delia's party all over again?" asked Annette, and it was decided to do this just as Grandma Vincent and "Lion" drove up to the front door. But when Annette told her Grandmother of the plan for the birthday party Madame Vincent shook her head.

"I have a much better idea. I am going to have a party myself on the first day of September, and I have already invited Delia, Betty, Isabel and the Van Steldt twins, with the five little asylum girls, and I expect you and Nancy to come over the evening before and stay the night," she said, smiling down at Nancy's happy face.

Both the little girls thought this a much finer plan than their own, but as the time drew near to start for Greenwich Village Annette was so quiet and serious that Mrs. Vincent became troubled by her little daughter's sober face, and Nancy began to wonder if Annette was tired of her. The more Nancy thought about it the more sure she was that Annette no longer cared for her company.

"Annette looks at me without smiling, and when I say anything about September first she sighs and

looks unhappy; prob'ly she wants me to go back to
the 'sylum before then and is too good to say so,"
decided the homeless little girl, and on the day
before Mr. Vincent was to drive Annette and Nancy
to Greenwich Village Nancy made up her mind that
she must go back to the asylum.

"I guess I better go without talkin' 'bout it,"
decided the homeless child, "then when Annette
finds I'm gone she'll be glad."

This was no easy decision for Nancy. To leave this
place where everybody was kind, where little girls
were never scolded, but praised, and even kissed;
where there were such wonderful things to eat and
such pretty things to wear—to leave all this, and,
hardest of all, not to see Annette again, and to return
to the asylum where little girls were "seen but not
heard," was a great sacrifice for Nancy.

But they will take me back to the 'sylum after the
birthday, so I might as well go before, then Annette
can have it all for herself," thought Nancy, and as
night approached she made up her mind to slip away
as soon as Annette had gone to sleep.

The little girls went up to their room early that
night. Annette was very silent. She was thinking that
in two more days Nancy would have to return to the
asylum, and the thought made her unhappy. She had
asked her mother that very morning if she might not
ask Nancy to make a longer visit, and Mrs. Vincent

SHE WOULD CREEP OUT OF THE HOUSE

had said, "No, do not speak to Nancy about it," so Annette felt sure that after the birthday visit with Grandma she would have to say good-bye to Nancy and the thought made her unhappy. She realized that the little asylum girl had grown very dear to her, "even more dear than Kathy," she acknowledged.

"Good-night, Annette. Dear Annette," said Nancy as she sat up in the little bed and looked at the shadowy little figure in the bed so near her own. But Annette did not respond. She was nearly ready to sob out her unhappiness that Nancy must return to the asylum, so after a moment's silence, Nancy, with a little sigh of disappointment, laid her head on the pillow and waited for Annette to go to sleep. Nancy's doll lay beside her; the ugly grey cloth dress that she had worn when she came to the Cherry Street house hung in the closet where she could easily reach it. Her plan was made; she would slip on the grey dress, take the doll and creep out of the house and make her way back to the asylum. It was all she could do, she thought, for Annette, who had been so good to her.

An hour later and Nancy had carried out part of her plan. She had put on her grey dress and, with her doll closely clasped in her arm, had made her way down-stairs to the back door and out to the street without being discovered. She ran along the shadowy street unnoticed by the occasional passersby. But Nancy had not the slightest idea of where the asylum was. The building where homeless children were sheltered stood on the outskirts of the city. Nancy's only thought was to get as far from Annette as possible.

"When she wakes up and finds I'm gone then she will be happy again," Nancy thought, with a little sob over all she was leaving behind her.

She turned from one street to another, stopping now and then to hide behind a tree until some little group of people had passed her, and finally growing so tired and footsore that she resolved to rest, and looked about her anxiously and found herself in front of a fine brick mansion, whose broad steps came to the sidewalk. There were lights in the upper rooms, but the doorway was dark, and Nancy decided it would be the very place to rest, and her bare feet made no noise as she slowly mounted the steps and curled up in the darkest corner of the doorway.

CHAPTER XVI

NANCY VINCENT

NANCY was very tired, and although she had meant to rest only for a moment she at once went fast asleep, and did not awaken until the next morning when the servant of Adjutant-General De Lancey opened the front door and stared in surprise at the frightened child who scrambled to her feet and would have fled down the steps had the man not grasped her by the arm.

"What are you doing here?" he questioned. Before Nancy could reply a voice called from the hallway, "Who is your early visitor, Jacobs ?" and General Oliver De Lancey himself, in the fine uniform of a British General, stood in the doorway.

"Who is the child?" he asked, and then said: "Whoever she is, take her into the house, Jacobs, and give her a good breakfast. Tell your wife to take care of her and find out where she belongs," and the General hurried down the steps, while Jacobs led Nancy, still too frightened to speak, into the house.

It was an hour later before Annette awoke to find herself alone in the pleasant chamber, but the fact that Nancy was not in bed did not alarm her. She supposed Nancy had dressed quietly and gone down-stairs, and not until she was ready for breakfast and had called Nancy's name from the back porch and run up-stairs to make sure that the little girl was not there did she begin to wonder what had befallen her; but when Mrs. Vincent discovered that Nancy's grey dress and doll were gone, although none of the things given to the little asylum girl during her visit had disappeared, she was sure Nancy had returned to her former home.

"But what for?" Annette questioned tearfully. "We were to go to Grandma's this very day, and to-morrow was our birthday. Why would Nancy want to leave us?"

Mrs. Vincent could not answer this question, and did her best to comfort Annette, who did not want her breakfast and could hardly wait for her father to get ready to drive to the asylum and bring Nancy back, or discover why she did not wish to remain at the Cherry Street house.

Annette was in the chaise before her father and mother reached the street, and as they drove along her mother told her of a birthday surprise they had planned for the two little girls.

"It was all settled for Nancy to live with us until she was eighteen years of age," said Mrs. Vincent, "and she was to be called Nancy Vincent, and to be taught to become a useful woman. We were going to tell you to-morrow morning."

But Annette could not wait for her mother to say another word. Her face brightened and she exclaimed happily: "Just as if Nancy were my real sister! Oh, Mother, what a splendid birthday present!"

"But it is evident that Nancy does not want to stay with us; she has returned to the asylum," Mrs. Vincent reminded Annette.

"But there is some other reason. I know Nancy wanted to stay with us," Annette insisted so eagerly that Mr. and Mrs. Vincent were soon convinced that their little daughter was right, although they could not understand Nancy's disappearance. When they discovered that the little girl was not at the asylum they became sure that Nancy must be at the Cherry Street house, and the matron of the asylum assured them that Nancy would not go far from a place where she had been so contented and happy, and they turned toward home, confident of finding the missing girl.

But Nancy was being taken excellent care of at the De Lancey mansion by Mrs. Jacobs, who had decided that the little waif was dumb, as Nancy had not spoken since the puzzled servants had taken her to their quarters in the rear of the house. She would nod soberly, or shake her head when they questioned her, and held her doll closely when Mrs. Jacobs told her to sit in the back garden, "where I can keep my eye on you," said the perplexed woman.

But as the day passed Nancy became more and more unhappy, and when Mrs. Jacobs called her to come in for her dinner she turned and ran through the garden toward the street, and was nearly run over by two soldiers on horseback, who quickly drew rein, and one of them exclaimed:

" 'Tis the child I found on my steps this morning," and De Lancey looked questioningly down at the forlorn little girl.

John Van Arsdale, hurrying along the street toward Bowling Green, wondered to himself what had caused Adjutant-General De Lancey and his lieutenant to draw rein so suddenly, and then he saw Nancy and sprang forward.

"What are you doing here, Nancy? " he asked. "I have just come from Cherry Street and they are searching everywhere for you."

"Take the girl back where she belongs," said De Lancey, and rode on. John looked after him scornfully. For although De Lancey wore a British uniform, he had been born in America, and was therefore despised by loyal Americans because of his allegiance to the English king.

As John hurried Nancy toward home she sobbed out her belief that Annette did not want her to stay for the birthday party, and told of spending the night in the doorway of the De Lancey mansion.

It would be difficult to say which of the two little girls was the happier when Nancy appeared at the door of the Cherry Street house and Annette came running to welcome her, while John told the story of Nancy's disappearance, adding a word as to his opinion of Oliver De Lancey. Mr. and Mrs. Vincent now told the little girl of their wish that she should henceforth make her home with them, and when Annette told Nancy that she had been afraid that after the birthday Nancy would return to the asylum the last doubt left the child's heart and she chattered happily as the two little girls ran upstairs to make ready for the ride to Greenwich Village. Nancy never again doubted her welcome in her new home.

Just before leaving her room that morning, Annette opened the lower drawer of the highboy and took out the package Kathy had sent her.

"I will take this and open it to-morrow, just as Kathy asked me to," she said, and the little box was put carefully into the bag Annette was taking to Greenwich Village.

No more was said of Nancy's runaway adventure, and none of the happy party who arrived at the "Farm in the Woods" on the following day ever knew that the smiling, happy Nancy, who they were told was now to be called Nancy Vincent, and was to live in the Vincent family, had spent an entire night on the steps of the De Lancey house.

Early on the morning of September first Annette crept from her bed in the big front chamber at

Grandma Vincent's house and unwrapped the little package Kathy had given her and found a beautiful beaded purse.

"Oh, this is the very one Kathy asked me to set a stitch in that day I was at her house, and I wouldn't because I thought she was making it for Sir Guy Carleton, and 'twas for me all the time," thought Annette, as she looked at her friend's lovely gift. On one side of the purse the letter "A" was worked in gold beads, while on the other side was a wonderful pink rose. Inside the purse was a slip of white paper on which was written: " To Annette with Kathy's love."

While Nancy and Annette were eating breakfast "Lion" kept running to a closed door and barking angrily.

"What is the matter with 'Lion,' Grandma?" questioned Annette, but Grandma only said that "Lion" was jealous, a reply that puzzled both Annette and Nancy until Marrilla opened the closet door and two little fat white dogs came jumping out.

"Oh, Grandma!" exclaimed Annette, and when Madame Vincent smiled and said, "Yes, my dears, they are your birthday presents," instantly Annette picked up one of the white puppies and Nancy the other, while "Lion" ran to Mrs. Vincent, as if expecting a word of comfort.

Before the little girls could decide upon names for their new possessions there was the sound of wheels on the driveway and they all ran to welcome the other guests. Milly was delighted to see Nancy again, and the two little girls ran off to the garden to tell each other all that had happened since Nancy left the asylum. Then Annette led the way to the stables and introduced all her friends to " Sir Guy," the colt, and the September day passed quickly, and when late in the afternoon Grimm announced that the big wagon was ready to take the girls back to New York the little white dogs had not yet been named.

As each of her little guests bade Madame Vincent good-bye and thanked her for their pleasant day she handed each girl a small package. "To remember the Vincent girls' birthday by," she said smilingly, and her guests curtseyed again, and again thanked her. Even the awkward little girls from the asylum did their best to imitate the graceful manners of "the other six."

As the big wagon with its happy passengers rolled along Greenwich Lane and then homeward along the river road the girls suggested names for the little white dogs and before Bowling Green was reached Nancy's dog was named "Star" and Annette's was named "Glory," because Delia had declared the puppy to be a glorious dog.

Each of the asylum girls was to stay that night with her special friend, and Grimm left them all safely at their homes. When he drove up to the Cherry

Street house the stars were already shining in the clear September sky and Nancy was so sleepy that Grimm lifted her from the wagon and carried her, with "Star," her doll and the little package that she held so tightly, up the steps.

As she again found herself in the pleasant chamber from which she had fled the previous night, never expecting to return, Nancy looked about with grateful eyes.

"Nancy Vincent. Nancy Vincent," she whispered happily. Annette heard the whisper, and she too smiled happily, well pleased with the gifts that her eleventh birthday had brought. She named them over as she made ready for bed. "The lovely purse that Kathy made on purpose for me, and Nancy to stay right here till she grows up, and the pretty work-bag, and Glory—" and before she had really finished the list her eyes closed and she was fast asleep.

CHAPTER XVII

ANNETTE IN PERIL

"ANNETTE, I want you to tell me something!"

It was a week after the birthday party at Greenwich Village and Annette and Nancy were under the big tree near the landing. "Star" and "Glory" were playing happily near by. A large book rested on Annette's lap, at which Nancy had been looking intently, but as she asked the question she looked anxiously up at the older girl.

Annette nodded soberly. Since the discovery that poor little Nancy could not read Annette was eager to teach her, and to answer any question Nancy might ask. Annette was quite sure that a girl of eleven years was very nearly a young lady when compared to a little girl only eight years old.

"Annette," and Nancy's voice grew even more serious than at first, "what is a 'patriot'? Your Cousin John is always talking about being a 'patriot.' What is it? Am I one?"

For a moment Annette was puzzled as to the reply she would make. She was quite sure that she knew the true meaning of the word. To Annette "patriot" meant a person who was loyal to America and its good,

169

and who was willing to suffer, as her own father had done, to protect his country from an enemy. But she did not know exactly how to explain this to Nancy.

"Well, Nancy, you see, you were born in America, so that makes you a patriot," she began, and then remembering Oliver De Lancey, who had turned against his native land, and Benedict Arnold, who had betrayed his country to the enemy, she added quickly: "There are always two kinds, Nancy. Good Americans are patriots, and bad Americans are traitors," and Nancy was quite ready to accept this explanation.

This morning they were waiting for John to come sailing up to the landing in the *Fleetwing* and take them for a cruise about the harbor. Lottie had promised to look after "Star" and "Glory" while the little girls were away, and to protect the little white dogs from the ill-tempered cat, "Matilda," who refused to make friends with the newcomers.

Annette had just closed the book from which she had been giving Nancy her reading lesson when the *Fleetwing* came sailing up to the landing.

"A fine breeze," John declared, as he helped the girls on board, "and I have a message for Captain James Duncan at Governor's Island, so we'll sail straight down if this fair wind will hold." John smiled a little mischievously at Annette's puzzled look.

"Why shouldn't I call on Captain Duncan if you can visit Sir Guy Carleton?" he asked. "They are both British officers."

Annette's face flushed. "You know I had to go, John," she responded quickly, and was about to remind her cousin of the promise the British General had made her when John continued: "As it happens, I am not going as a visitor. I have a letter for Captain Duncan from Governor George Clinton himself."

This was astonishing news and Annette's face brightened to think that she should be in the very boat that carried a message from the Governor of New York.

"What is it, John?" she asked eagerly.

John shook his head. "Squire Kipp did not say. He only gave me the sealed envelope and bade me take good care to deliver it to Captain Duncan before noon," John answered; "but likely enough 'tis to tell the Britisher to make ready to clear the island at once. 'Tis weeks now since Sir Guy had word to leave this harbor, but his men and ships are still here."

Annette could not keep her eyes from the white paper that showed its edge above the top of John's pocket. "What would happen," she wondered, "if John should lose that letter?" And while each little girl's thoughts were busy with these things John's eyes were fixed ahead on the shores of the historic Governor's Island, that had been purchased from the Indians in 1637 by the West India Company, and which had been captured by the British forces in 1776, and was still held by them. John was well pleased to be the bearer of what he was sure was an important message, and now and then he would touch his pocket to make sure of the safety of the letter that Squire Kipp, a friend of Washington, had intrusted to him.

The September morning had been warm and sunny, but as the *Fleetwing* made its way toward Governor's Island a cold wind came over the water, and the little girls were glad to wrap their blue flannel capes about them, and John moved quickly forward to reef the big sail. As he started up his foot caught in a coil of rope and before he could save himself he had pitched forward, the letter flying from his pocket as he fell.

Annette sprang after it as it fluttered toward her and grasped it just before it went over the boat's side, but the *Fleetwing* at that moment keeled over dangerously, and Annette lost her balance and fell into the water.

John had now struggled to his feet and cleared himself of the entangling rope. He hardly realized the great danger his little cousin was in until he saw that Nancy was hanging over the side of the boat holding with both hands to Annette's skirt, which the little girl had managed to grasp as her friend fell into the water.

It did not take John long to pull his cousin into the boat. She was still grasping the folded paper with its big seals, and even in her perilous tumble overboard, Annette had managed to keep the letter out of the water. Nancy had been so quick in grabbing at Annette's skirts and had held on so valiantly that, beyond a thorough wetting, she was none the worse for her successful effort to save the Governor's letter to Captain Duncan.

For a moment the little girls and John looked at each other in astonishment and then John, taking the letter from Annette's grasp, exclaimed: "How did you think to save it, Annette?"

"You said it was to make the British soldiers leave New York," Annette answered, "but I would have been drowned, letter and all, if Nancy had not grabbed my skirt and held me up."

"You must get out of those wet things. I have some old clothes in the cabin. Go in and put them on and we can dry your clothes," said John hastily, feeling a little ashamed of his own clumsiness that had come so near to the loss of an important paper and endangered Annette's life.

Annette and Nancy hurried into the tiny cabin and Annette was glad indeed to take off her wet clothing and slip into the old woolen blouse and trousers that she found rolled up on a shelf. For a moment both the little girls forgot the peril Annette had just escaped as they laughed at the queer little figure in the loose clumsy garments.

"You saved my life, Nancy," Annette said soberly, as she gathered up her skirts to take them on deck to dry,—"truly you did. If you had not held tight I would have gone under the water."

Nancy looked at her gratefully. The little asylum girl was even more happy than when told that her name was to be Nancy Vincent, for she had at last been able to do a service for Annette.

When the two girls came out of the tiny cabin John's face was very grave. He did not even smile at the queer little figure Annette presented in his old garments. He had been thinking of his own unfairness toward his little cousin because of her friendship for Tory Down's daughter, and her call to apologize to Sir Guy Carleton, and now Annette had saved him from he knew not what punishment and disgrace by rescuing Governor Clinton's letter that had been intrusted to him. So now John realized that he must own to his cousin that she had performed an important service.

"You were mighty brave, Annette, to risk a fall overboard to save that letter," he said, as his cousin took her old place beside him.

"But it would have been dreadful to have lost it," Annette responded.

"Indeed it would. For me, surely, and for all New York, for that matter. Why, Annette, you were as brave as an American soldier," declared John handsomely. "I'll never doubt your being loyal after this."

Annette flushed at her cousin's approval. She felt it was well worth a tumble into New York harbor to have John acknowledge that she was a loyal American, but she did not forget that but for Nancy's quick thought and ready help the letter would have been lost, and she said quickly:

"It was really Nancy who saved the letter, John. If

she had not held on to my skirt I would have been drowned."

"Nancy was plucky," declared John approvingly, and now they all talked over this unexpected adventure, and the little girls were well pleased when John said that it was fortunate for him that they had been on board.

They landed at the wharf at Governor's Island, where British officers and men were still on guard, but John had no trouble in finding Captain Duncan and delivering his message, while Annette and Nancy remained on board the *Fleetwing*.

As they sailed home, John said that he believed that it would now be a very short time before the English soldiers set sail for their own country. "The English captain was very polite to me," the boy said. "He no longer sneers at a message from an American governor of the State of New York," John added proudly.

As their boat passed the Battery, Annette looked up at the British flag floating from the tall flagpole.

"I'd like to be the one to pull down that flag when Sir Guy Carleton and his soldiers embark for England," declared John, as he, too, gazed at the emblem of America's conquered foe.

"Perhaps you will," said Annette seriously, and a few weeks later, with Annette's help, John Van Arsdale did indeed take down that very flag, although on the September day as the cousins gazed up at the flag neither of them would have believed that such wonderful good fortune could befall them.

As Annette's mother listened to the story of the rescue of Governor Clinton's letter and heard of Nancy's quickness and courage in springing to Annette's assistance and holding her until John could draw Annette into safety, Mrs. Vincent declared that she was proud of both the girls, but it was Nancy to whom she gave the greatest praise.

"You were very brave and strong, dear child, to hold on so courageously. I wonder you were not pulled overboard," she said, drawing Nancy closer and kissing her flushed cheek. "If you had not been with Annette I hardly dare think what might have befallen her."

Annette listened happily to her mother's approval of Nancy. "It's good luck to have Nancy live with us, isn't it, Mother, dear?" she said, and Mrs. Vincent smilingly agreed.

"John said that by saving the Governor's letter I had served the American government," Annette added, "and now John believes me to be a loyal little maid, even if I am Kathy Down's true friend, and if I was polite to Sir Guy Carleton."

"Of course you are loyal as well as brave, my dear, and your cousin has had proof of it," responded Mrs. Vincent, greatly to Annette's satisfaction, and as the two little girls started off to tell Lottie of the day's adventures, she thought to herself that it was indeed good fortune that had given Annette so unselfish a friend as Nancy.

CHAPTER XVIII

SEPTEMBER passed quickly, and October came with its crimson leaves and cool days, and Annette and Nancy now spent many happy hours in the big pleasant kitchen, where Lottie was only too glad to teach them how to mix the dough for sugar cookies, to roll it out on the smooth cake-board and cut the rounds or squares that came out of the oven crisp and spicy.

Every day Mr. Vincent brought news of the movements of British troops preparing to embark for England, and the household of the Cherry Street home, like that of every American household in New York, waited eagerly for the day when General George Washington and his loyal soldiers should again march triumphantly into the city from which they had been driven by the superior forces of the English in 1776.

Although many things had happened since Merchant Down sailed away for Bermuda, Annette had not forgotten her promise to write to her little Tory friend, and she had written a number of pages telling Kathy of Delia's birthday surprise, of "the other six," and of Nancy, and the fact that the little asylum girl was henceforth to be called Nancy

Vincent, and this letter was to be finished and sealed as soon as John should bring Annette word of any vessel leaving New York for Bermuda.

Annette waited hopefully for a letter from Kathy. She was sure that Kathy had not forgotten her, and that a letter would arrive perhaps when she least expected it.

But October passed, and November, with its chilly rains and cold winds, came and there was no letter from Kathy, and the British troops still lingered, but Annette heard her father say that at last a day had been set for their departure. "The greatest day New York has ever seen will be Thursday, November the twenty-fifth, 1783," Mr. Vincent declared, "for that is the day when General George Washington and Governor Clinton will arrive in New York, and when the British fleet will sail out of the harbor."

Annette listened eagerly to all her father said about the preparations being made to welcome General Washington, and Mr. Vincent promised his little daughter that she should see the fine procession when it marched from the Bowery to the Battery. Grandma Vincent would drive in from Greenwich Village for the great celebration. Every day saw the Tory inhabitants leaving New York with their movable possessions, and exiled Americans returning to the city.

Annette and Nancy were busy making "Union Cockades," of black and white ribbon, that all loyal

Americans were to wear, with a sprig of laurel, on their left breast and on their hats on the day when they should welcome Washington to New York. Delia and Betty came to the Cherry Street house one afternoon a few days before the great day, and Delia, as usual, had a plan to suggest.

"I think all the children at the asylum ought to have a fine dinner on the day the British leave the city, and all be dressed up and brought to Bowling Green to see General Washington and his troops, then they will always remember it," and Delia looked from Betty to Annette as if sure they could settle the question by their approval, but it was Nancy who spoke first.

"Oh, that would be splendid! You girls don't know what it is to live in a 'sylum—" Nancy stopped suddenly. She was afraid she would cry if she told these kind, pleasant and friendly girls about the "other" girls who had no home or pleasures, and about whose happiness no one seemed to think except Delia Davidson and Annette.

"How could we manage it, Delia?" said Betty. "Only this morning my father said that the Tories were taking everything out of the city, and that provisions were hard to get."

"Oh, Betty, of course we can give the asylum girls a good dinner," declared Annette eagerly. "We can ask everybody to help us, to make cake and buns, to cook a chicken. Everybody who has a little girl of his own will want to help, I am sure they will."

"Yes," Betty agreed soberly, taking her knitting from the bag that she always carried over her arm. "And I suppose we can help dress them up. I have knit six pairs of good stockings since your birthday, Annette, and Nancy can give those to the six girls she likes best in the asylum," and Betty smiled at Nancy's exclamation of delight.

Delia declared that there was no time to lose if they were to carry out this plan.

"I'll hurry home and ask my father to go to the asylum and tell them our plan, and ask my mother to help," she said, and Betty agreed to do the same, while Annette and Nancy, after bidding their friends good-bye, ran to find Mrs. Vincent and tell her of Delia's wonderful plan for November twenty-fifth.

"It will mean a good deal of work, and you girls must do your part," said Mrs. Vincent.

"Yes, indeed we will. Oh, Mother, isn't Delia splendid?" responded Annette.

It was finally decided that Delia, Betty, Isabelle Clifton, Annette and Nancy, each one to be accompanied by one of the asylum girls, should go from house to house, tell her plan for November twenty-fifth and ask the assistance of the families upon whom they called to furnish a good dinner for the asylum children, and suitable clothing for them to wear for the great day.

Annette and Nancy, with Milly as their companion, started off on their errand the next morning. Milly was brought to the Cherry Street house and both Annette and Nancy were eager to dress Milly in such of their own garments as she could wear. A pair of the stockings Betty had knit just fitted Milly, and when the three little girls set forth Milly was as well dressed as either of her companions; her short hair was concealed by a pretty hood of brown cloth that Annette had given her, and the little asylum girl now and then smiled happily at Nancy as, hand in hand, they walked beside Annette to the door of Mr. Samuel Broom, who welcomed them and promised two fine turkeys and a bushel of apples as his contribution toward the dinner for the asylum children.

"And, if you please, sir, will you send the things at once?" suggested Annette, and Mr. Broom, who was one of the committee of citizens selected to escort General Washington on his entrance to the city, declared that no time should be lost before the turkeys and apples should be started for the asylum.

"Why, everybody wants to give," Annette declared to her little companions, as they went from door to door and were met everywhere with promises of help.

"There will be enough for two dinners," said Nancy, "and shoes for all the girls."

As they passed the Broadway Street house where the British Commander-in-Chief lived, Annette looked up at it and remembered the day in early summer when she had so reluctantly visited the house to ask Sir Guy's pardon for her want of courtesy, and recalled his friendly reception of the little American girl whom he had asked to try and think kindly of him.

The older people were astonished at the success the little girls achieved. The matron of the asylum declared that an abundance of food had been received, and that a feast was assured for all the asylum children. On November twenty-fourth Delia, Betty, Annette and Nancy went with Mrs. Vincent and a number of other ladies to the asylum carrying stockings, shoes, hoods and capes for the little girls to wear, and Nancy gave Betty's stockings to the little girls who had been her former playmates. Nancy was perhaps the happiest little girl in all the city of New York on the eve of the great day that was to see the British fleet sail out of New York harbor, never again to return. But that day was not to end without bringing a surprise to Annette.

They had just returned home from the visit to the asylum. Mr. and Mrs. Vincent had gone to consult with other friends about the celebration of the following day, and Annette and Nancy, with Lottie, were alone in the house when a loud knock at the front door echoed through the house, and Lottie came hurrying into the sitting-room, where the little girls were sitting on the rug before a cheerful open fire, saying in a whisper:

"Lan' sake, Miss Annette! Wot we gwine ter do? Dar's a British Sojer at de door a-askin' ter see yo'! He say he hab a message fer Miss Annette Vincent," and Lottie looked at her young mistress with frightened eyes.

"It must be for Father," Annette said, jumping up from the rug.

But Lottie shook her head. "No, Missie, he say som't'ing 'bout dat islan' place whar dose Tory fo'k go."

"Kathy! It's from Kathy!" exclaimed Annette eagerly, running toward the door, with Lottie close behind her.

The young English soldier smiled at Annette's eager question: "Have you brought me a letter from Kathy Down?" and responded:

"I hope so, little maid. Sir Guy Carleton sends you this package with his compliments, and bade me say that if you had any message for Miss Katherine Down to give it to me and that he would make sure that it reached her safely."

"Yes, yes, I have a letter all ready except sealing," said Annette, as she took the packet the soldier offered her. "Will you not come in while I get it ready?"

"Thank you, I will wait here," the soldier answered, and Annette sped up-stairs to scribble another brief word to Kathy and then seal the letter which was to go to her little Tory friend, and in a few moments she was back at the door and the soldier had taken the missive.

"Please tell Sir Guy that I thank him very much, and I thank you, too," said Annette with a little curtsey.

"I am glad to do you a service, little maid," the young soldier replied, and touching his cap he ran down the steps, while Annette hurried back to the sitting-room to read Kathy's long expected letter.

The morning of November twenty-fifth, 1783, dawned clear and fine, and the British troops, who had so long encamped along the Bowery, began to march toward the Battery and embark on the waiting ships. As these soldiers left their various posts their places were taken by Americans, and New York was soon quietly in the possession of the American army. At noon General Henry Knox, with a great number of respectable citizens on horseback, repaired to the Bowery to meet General Washington and Governor Clinton and escort them to the city. It was to be a great procession, and New York's streets were filled with happy people eager to do honor to the great Washington, whose wisdom and valor had led America to her rightful freedom.

Annette and Nancy with Mrs. Vincent and Grandma Vincent, in Grandma's comfortable carriage, driven by Grimm, were at Bowling Green in good season, and the little girls waved their hands at the asylum girls, who were there before them, all smiling with delight at the wonderful holiday and eagerly pointing out to each other Delia, Annette and Betty, as the girls who had given them so great a treat.

Shortly after one o'clock loud huzzas were heard from the crowds at the Battery, and the people realized that the last British soldier had embarked, and now cheers echoed along the streets, and marching into the city came His Excellency George Washington and Governor George Clinton, with their respective suites, and followed by senators, the officers of the army and citizens on horseback, marching eight abreast. As the worn troops in their shabby uniforms moved along the streets so lately vacated by the well-cared-for and brilliantly dressed British soldiers, many of the older people felt as if they were beholding the greatest event in America's history.

Grimm skilfully made his way toward the Battery and on one of the side streets Grandma and Mrs. Vincent and the little girls left the carriage and hurried to the Battery, where the triumphant march was to end.

Annette glanced quickly toward the tall flagpole.

"Oh, the British flag is still there!" she exclaimed, and at the same moment Washington and his companions approached the Battery, and it was discovered that the British flag, in parting defiance, had been nailed to the flagstaff, the halliards unreefed, the cleats knocked off, and the pole greased to prevent climbing.

"Where is John? Oh, where is John? He could climb that pole," exclaimed Annette, and suddenly remembered that it had been several days since she had seen her cousin. Every second brought Washington nearer, and to the little girl, as to everyone waiting at the Battery, it seemed a dreadful thing that the British flag should float there as he approached.

Annette made a resolve that she must find her cousin. Surely John must be near at such a time, and she looked anxiously about for some sign of him. John was a sailor who could climb anywhere, she thought, and in a moment she had slipped away from her mother's side and was running toward the shore. "John may have sailed to the Battery," she thought, as she made her way among the crowd and came to the edge of the pier.

Yes. There lay the *Fleetwing*, just far enough distant for John to watch the great happenings on shore, but too far away to hear Annette's voice as she called his name.

Annette snatched off her blue cape and waved it frantically. "Oh, why doesn't he see me!" Annette exclaimed, and why did John not see that the flag he had so long wished to pull down still floated above loyal Americans, and that at any moment might float above Washington himself? And John had seen the flag, but believed that it was to be the privilege of some favorable American to furl it.

But at last Annette's calls caught her cousin's attention, and believing that the little girl was in some danger and needed his assistance, he instantly headed his boat for the landing-place and in a few moments was on shore. But before he could make the *Fleetwing* fast Annette was beside him.

"John! John! That flag, the British flag, is nailed to the pole. Nobody can get it. I saw men try and they couldn't. You can—" But before Annette could finish John had turned and was racing toward the flagpole. His sailor's training now stood him in good stead. By the time he reached the flagpole he had determined just what must be done. With a pocketful of sand he knew he could climb up that tall staff.

"I can haul down that flag. Nail on a couple of cleats here and give me a hand up," he called to the excited group, "and fetch a pail of sand," he ordered a small boy, who sped away instantly and was back by the time the first cleats were nailed on.

Then up went John toward the top of the pole, while a hush fell on the waiting crowd and nearer and nearer came the music that sounded the approach of the Commander of the American army.

Annette had run after her cousin and now stood watching him with clasped hands and an anxious heart.

"Oh, if he slips; if he doesn't get to the top, what can we do?" whispered the little girl, who for the moment had forgotten everything except that the flag of England still floated as if in triumph while America's emblem was not in its rightful place.

But John went steadily on, and as he tore the flag from its halliards and nailed the American flag in its place a great cheer rose from the crowd, and friends who had recognized John shouted his name triumphantly. The British ships were going slowly down the bay, but they were sure to have their glasses turned toward the Battery and to have seen the disappearance of their flag.

And now General Washington and his distinguished company had reached the Battery, and as John Van Arsdale stood at the foot of the flagpole eager hands seized him, and the boy was nearly carried to the side of the great General's horse, while the story of the flags and John's part in raising the emblem of America was briefly described. But as Washington smiled approvingly on the lad and added his word of commendation, that John was to treasure all his life, the boy exclaimed: " 'Tis my cousin Annette you should praise, sir, if you please. For 'twas she who bade me climb the flagpole," and John looked quickly about for his small cousin, and seeing her not far away he pointed toward her.

"There she is, with the blue cape." A tall man standing beside Annette bent toward her, and lifting the astonished little girl in his arms carried her toward General Washington.

"Set me down, quickly, if you please, sir, that I may curtsey to the great Washington," said Annette, and with a little laugh her tall friend set Annette on her feet beside her Cousin John, who held out his hand in welcome.

"If you please, sir, this is my cousin, Annette Vincent, who bade me climb the flagpole," said John, and Annette made her best curtsey as Washington leaned toward them and said:

"You are brave and loyal children, and I am proud that a little maid of New York should be so eager to see America's flag float over her native city."

John bowed low and Annette curtseyed again, and General Washington and his staff turned and moved back toward the hotel where they were to dine.

Hand in hand the cousins hurried in search of Annette's mother, and John again told the story of his cousin's search for him and of what had followed.

"Was she not a loyal little maid to want that flag down?" questioned John, as if forgetful of his own great part in the greatest event of the most important day in the history of New York.

Delia and Betty came running to speak with Annette, eager to hear the exact words that General Washington had said, and as the girls walked toward Cherry Street it was Delia who recalled that day in June when John had taken Annette and her friends for the picnic to Staten Island. "And John said that very day that he would like to be the one to pull down the British flag from the Battery flagpole, and now he has pulled it down," said Delia triumphantly.

"But I would not have had the chance if it had not been for Annette," John declared, with an approving smile at his cousin.

Far down the harbor the ships of the British fleet were now nearly out of sight and the little group stood for a moment for a last look at them.

"Good-bye Sir Guy," Annette whispered to herself, in remembrance of her promise to give the British General a friendly thought when he should sail away from America. Then she recalled the kindly words of Washington as he had smiled down upon her. "'A loyal little maid of New York,'" General Washington had called her, and Annette's great desire was at last fulfilled, for now her Cousin John was quite ready to agree with General Washington and would never again doubt Annette's loyalty.

The Stories in This Series Are:

A LITTLE MAID OF PROVINCETOWN
A LITTLE MAID OF MASSACHUSETTS COLONY
A LITTLE MAID OF NARRAGANSETT BAY
A LITTLE MAID OF OLD PHILADELPHIA
A LITTLE MAID OF OLD NEW YORK
A LITTLE MAID OF OLD CONNECTICUT
A LITTLE MAID OF TICONDEROGA
A LITTLE MAID OF VIRGINIA
A LITTLE MAID OF MARYLAND
A LITTLE MAID OF MOHAWK VALLEY